Living On One Day's Rations

**First Lesson Sermons
For Sundays After Pentecost
(Middle Third)**

Cycle A

Douglas B. Bailey

CSS Publishing Company, Inc., Lima, Ohio

LIVING ON ONE DAY'S RATIONS

Copyright © 2001 by
CSS Publishing Company, Inc.
Lima, Ohio

All rights reserved. No part of this publication may be reproduced in any manner whatsoever without the prior permission of the publisher, except in the case of brief quotations embodied in critical articles and reviews. Inquiries should be addressed to: Permissions, CSS Publishing Company, Inc., P.O. Box 4503, Lima, Ohio 45802-4503.

Scripture quotations are from the *New Revised Standard Version of the Bible*, copyright 1989 by the Division of Christian Education of the National Council of the Churches of Christ in the USA. Used by permission.

Library of Congress Cataloging-in-Publication Data

Bailey, Douglas B., 1935-
　Living on one day's rations : first lesson sermons for Sundays after Pentecost (middle third), cycle A / Douglas B. Bailey.
　　p. cm.
　ISBN 0-7880-1820-5 (alk. paper)
　1. Pentecost season—Sermons. 2. Sermons, American. I. Title.
BV4300.5 .B35 2001
252'.64—dc21　　　　　　　　　　　　　　　　　　　　　　　　　2001025075
　　　　　　　　　　　　　　　　　　　　　　　　　　　　　　　　　　　　CIP

For more information about CSS Publishing Company resources, visit our website at www.csspub.com.

ISBN 0-7880-1820-5　　　　　　　　　　　　　　　　　　　　PRINTED IN U.S.A.

This book is dedicated in gratitude to:

*my father, Francis L. Bailey,
for whom the Bible was his daily guide
and source of inner strength, and*

*my mother, Nina B. Bailey,
for whom church music was her special
pathway to the presence of God*

Table Of Contents

Introduction 7

Proper 12 9
Pentecost 10
Ordinary Time 17
    A Prize Worth Waiting For — Or Worth Working For?
    Genesis 29:15-28

Proper 13 15
Pentecost 11
Ordinary Time 18
    An Honest And Painful Wrestling Match
    Genesis 32:22-31

Proper 14 21
Pentecost 12
Ordinary Time 19
    When Life Is The Pits!
    Genesis 37:1-4, 12-28

Proper 15 27
Pentecost 13
Ordinary Time 20
    When It Hurts To Forgive
    Genesis 45:1-15

Proper 16 33
Pentecost 14
Ordinary Time 21
    Nothing Left But A Baby In A Basket
    Exodus 1:8—2:10

Proper 17   41
Pentecost 15
Ordinary Time 22
    I Really Am Who I Am!
    Exodus 3:1-15

Proper 18   47
Pentecost 16
Ordinary Time 23
    Saved Through The Blood Of The Lamb
    Exodus 12:1-14

Proper 19   55
Pentecost 17
Ordinary Time 24
    Coming Through In The Clutch
    Exodus 14:19-31

Proper 20   61
Pentecost 18
Ordinary Time 25
    Living On One Day's Rations
    Exodus 16:2-15

Proper 21   69
Pentecost 19
Ordinary Time 26
    Does God Help Those Who Help Themselves?
    Exodus 17:1-7

Proper 22   75
Pentecost 20
Ordinary Time 27
    When God Is Not "User Friendly"
    Exodus 20:1-4, 7-9, 12-20

Lectionary Preaching After Pentecost   83

Introduction

The sections on Genesis and Exodus in *The Interpreter's Bible* and *The New Interpreter's Bible* and various articles in *The Interpreter's Bible Dictionary* were the major biblical research sources consulted in preparing to write these ten sermons. Scriptural quotations were taken from the New Revised Standard Version of the Bible. These quotations were modified as necessary in the interests of inclusive language. The title "Prayer of Our Savior," as used in the Book of Worship for the United Church of Christ, was substituted for the traditional "Lord's Prayer." For the sake of a congregation's being able to identify the familiar first line of the hymn "How Firm A Foundation," the term "Lord" was allowed to remain in a direct quotation from this hymn. However, if desired, a suitable paraphrase could be "our God."

The author's style of preaching is to use a complete manuscript with vocabulary and sentence structure intended to meet the demands of "oral English." The reader's assessment of the merit and content of these sermons has to include reacting to "how this material sounds when it is read out loud." Since time spent in preaching should not induce the congregation to take a nap, the length of each sermon manuscript to be taken into the pulpit was strictly limited to six double spaced pages.

The reader will discover that the tenth sermon "Does God Help Those Who Help Themselves?" draws heavily upon material from Numbers 20 as well as from Exodus 17:1-17, the assigned lectionary text. This was done so that the basic theme of the tenth sermon could become more than just a "repeat" of what already has been covered in the ninth sermon "Living On One Day's Rations." The lectionary texts, Exodus 16:2-15 ("manna from heaven") and Exodus 17:1-17 ("water from the rock"), both are intended to point out the failure of the Israelites in the wilderness to trust God to provide for their basic survival needs. Reference is made in the tenth sermon to the Numbers account of Moses' disobedience to God in striking the rock (instead of commanding the rock to yield water) so that in addition to the Exodus theme of the Israelites' lack of faith, it is possible to bring up an issue raised by the Numbers account — namely, that when we lack faith and patience to trust God to take timely action to meet our urgent needs, we may be tempted to take matters into our own hands through impetuous decisions and actions. We then justify our impetuous behavior by rationalizing that "God helps those who help themselves." Biblical research for Numbers relied upon the sections on Numbers in *The Interpreter's Bible* and *The New Interpreter's Bible*.

Effort has been made in these ten sermons to emphasize strongly the current day relevance of ten well-known stories from the Old Testament. There is, regretfully, a tendency or temptation at times in so-called "lectionary based" preaching to give the congregation an extensive "Bible talk" with only casual or general reference to the congregation's personal concerns and life situations. The author has tried in these sermons to apply biblical content to some very specific, down-to-earth questions and concerns, plus provide a biblical and theological framework to help listeners cope with their "faith struggles."

**Proper 12
Pentecost 10
Ordinary Time 17
Genesis 29:15-28**

A Prize Worth Waiting For
— Or Worth Working For?

Is a wife worth waiting for or worth working for? Jacob put in a total of fourteen years working for his uncle Laban because he was in love with Laban's daughter, Rachel, and he felt she was indeed worth waiting for and worth working for. The original bargain was that Jacob would work a total of seven years and be rewarded by getting Rachel to be his wife. However, Laban had other ideas: he wanted to get his older daughter Leah married off first. Since Leah was less attractive than her younger sister Rachel, Laban pulled a fast one on Jacob by substituting Leah for Rachel as the bride whose face was concealed by the wedding veil. Jacob did not discover until it was too late that he had been joined to Leah and not Rachel in marriage. However, back in those days when a man could have more than one wife, Laban agreed to let Jacob take Rachel also as a wife if Jacob would put in seven more years tending Laban's herds of sheep, goats, and cattle. Laban, the sly old fox, says to Jacob, "You just have to understand, young feller, it just isn't the way things are done around here to let the youngest daughter be married before the first born. But look at it this way! We have a whole week of wedding celebration coming up. So just don't get upset now! Just enjoy yourself this week, help yourself to the food and drink, and then I'll let you have Rachel at the end of the week, with, of course, your agreement to give me seven more years of your time out in the fields!"

Have you ever been in a fix where you strike a deal, carry out your part of the bargain, and then are told that your part of the bargain is just not good enough? Perhaps you are on vacation and your car breaks down, and the mechanic says, "If you leave your car for two days, we'll have it fixed and running for you." So you do your sightseeing by bus or on foot or by rental car, and you come back to the garage two days later only to find your car's engine suspended high up in the air, and the mechanic says, "Sorry, we couldn't get certain parts delivered from out of town, and it's going to cost you more money than what we figured, but just give us two more days and we'll have you ready to hit the road!" Is your car worth waiting for, and do you feel you have no other choice but to cough up extra cash and extra time?

Or perhaps you have been told by your employer that if you work a certain number of years, you can retire with a guaranteed pension and adequate health benefits. So you put in your time and you carefully make your plans how you will have your mortgage paid off and all your kids put through college before you must pick up your pension and begin to learn how to live on less money and still do all the things you have always dreamed of doing. But then comes an unexpected surprise, a real shocker — your company now wants its older employees to take early retirement and accept a buy-out plan. Or here comes another unexpected event — your company now switches its health insurance coverage to another carrier with benefits that can equal what you have had all along, only if you cough up big extra dollars for health insurance premiums out of every pay check. Can you accept the retirement buy-out or pay the increased cost of health insurance, after the rules of the game have been changed in midstream unexpectedly, and there's no way you can turn back the clock and start all over again? A lot of things can happen, often through no fault of your own, so that you're forced to go the extra mile far beyond what you originally bargained for.

At first glance we might feel really sorry for poor, poor Jacob working fourteen long years out in the fields instead of seven, because to him Rachel was indeed worth waiting for and worth working for. But further investigation will show we can't really feel completely sorry for someone who got exactly what he deserved. The writers of the Old Testament stories about Jacob would want us to understand that in Jacob's case, he had it coming to him!

First of all, Jacob had outsmarted and finagled his older brother Esau into giving up the older brother's birthright to Jacob in exchange for a hot meal to relieve Esau's terrible hunger. Secondly, Jacob and his mother Rebekah tricked his father Isaac, old and blind on his deathbed, to bestow on Jacob the father's final blessing which normally would go to Esau as the oldest son. This final blessing would now make Jacob and not Esau become the powerful head of the family with all the tremendous privileges and prerogatives that went along with being the head honcho. The smooth-skinned and smooth-talking Jacob put on his brother's smelly clothes and carefully covered over his smooth skin with hairy animal hides which, to the hands of the blind Isaac, felt like the hairy skin of Esau, his oldest son, the son to whom Isaac wanted to give his final blessing. When Esau discovered how he had been cheated out of his father's blessing, he wanted to kill Jacob. So Jacob had to run for his life, far, far away to stay with his mother's brother, his uncle Laban. Before we feel completely sorry for poor, poor Jacob who had to put in fourteen years of hard labor for his shrewd uncle, we need to understand that Jacob had it coming to him! For in many ways it was truly a fitting touch of poetic justice and divine justice that Jacob ended up marrying Leah, the older sister whose face was hidden under the wedding veil in order to fool Jacob. When we consider how Jacob had hidden his own identity with a cover-up disguise of animal skins to trick Isaac, well — as the old saying goes — "Turn about is fair play!"

The story of Jacob raises for us today some disturbing questions. What in life is still worth waiting for or worth working for when an unpleasant surprise comes our way and we suddenly discover that the necessary conditions, demands, requirements, and costs of something we dearly want have gotten way out of hand — well beyond what we originally bargained for? It's not a quick or easy decision you can make, for example, if your house has been hit by an earthquake, a flood, or a tornado. Even if you have adequate insurance, will you then choose to rebuild and continue living in a section of the country that has a repeated history of nature's nightmares? When a teenager is getting more and more unreasonable and more and more unruly, just how far out on a limb do you go with patience and persistence? Just how deep in your pockets do you go, shelling out big money for counselors and therapists? Is tough love or tender love the answer which can make the vital difference?

When you turn to your Bible for peace and comfort and guidance for tough decisions, you will find that the Bible is full of examples of how the so-called "good people" are expected to go the extra mile for a God who always seems to go the extra mile for the so-called "bad people," the so-called "lost sheep" who really don't deserve having any shepherd leave the 99 good sheep in their safe quarters, while the shepherd risks his neck looking for the one wayward sheep that has gotten lost and waylaid. What can seem truly amazing to us about the story of Jacob is that in spite of his outrageous behavior as a deceitful wheeler and dealer, God blesses Jacob and selects him to be God's chosen instrument in the Great Shepherd's plan to create on the face of the earth a flock of faithful followers who are the direct descendants of a scheming scoundrel.

What the writers of the Old Testament want us to understand is that although Jacob was certainly no saint, he was in God's eyes a "diamond in the rough," someone whose spiritual growing pains and whose leadership capabilities sooner or later could make him able to preserve and pass on the spiritual heritage of Abraham and Isaac. But the story of Jacob and his descendants is not a story of God letting good things happen to so-called bad people, in order to let the so-called bad people get away with murder. Jacob and the people of Israel experienced tremendous growing pains, as they learned the hard way over a long period of time what God required of them. Justice begins to catch up with Jacob, when the clever rascal who had gotten the best of his father and his brother now has been tricked and outsmarted by his uncle. Because Jacob prefers Rachel and despises Leah, the Old Testament tells us that God sees to it that Leah is blessed by having children while Rachel is barren for several years before she ever has a child. Indeed, Jacob experiences enormous grief and pain when his beloved Rachel dies giving birth to Benjamin, and again years later when Jacob's favorite son, Joseph, is sold by his brothers as a slave to be taken to Egypt.

And Jacob is utterly terrified by the prospect of facing his brother Esau once again, when Jacob has to leave his uncle Laban's country and return home. He learns that Esau is on his way to meet him accompanied by a host of 400 men. Jacob, the rascal, who had once given his brother a measly dish of hot food in exchange for a birthright will go home to meet Esau face to face only after first sending a whopping present of 200 female goats, twenty male goats, 200 ewes, twenty rams, thirty camels and their young, forty cows, ten bulls, twenty female donkeys and ten male donkeys — absolutely no comparison whatsoever to the measly dish of hot food Jacob had cooked over a campfire in exchange for Esau's birthright. All of Jacob's grief and suffering are regarded in later Jewish tradition as the heavy price Jacob must pay for the terrible grief he caused his brother Esau. Eventually Jacob pays a heavy penalty for being a self-centered, slippery, smooth-talking sinner. The fourteen years that Jacob spent in Laban's fields were really only a small part of God's long-range plan that Jacob would go through many growing pains and learn the hard way again and again what God required of him as the patriarch entrusted with the spiritual heritage of Abraham and Isaac.

Like Jacob, most of us have had to learn the hard way what is worth waiting for and what is worth working for. It can be very hard to decide whether to wait for something better far ahead in the future or whether to settle instead for something right now we're really not crazy about. Instead of deciding that Rachel was indeed worth waiting for and worth working for, Jacob could have decided that seven more years was just too big a chunk out of his life to be gone from home any longer. He could have left his uncle Laban's country and headed for home, taking Leah, his new wife, with him. Instead of leaving our familiar hometown or our familiar place of employment for a promising situation which would require starting all over again — establishing a new group of friends, creating a new set of business customers or clients, finding, purchasing, and fixing up a new home — we could decide that the huge adjustment just isn't worth it, when the situation in our home town or our place of employment has gone definitely downhill but not to the point of being absolutely unbearable. We definitely may have second thoughts about making the move from a reasonably comfortable home where our yard has tall, well-established shade trees to a much more attractive home in a new housing development where we would have to start all over again from scratch and plant young saplings that would take years to get established.

Our Gospel lesson from Matthew has something valuable to teach us. It describes the dominion of heaven like a small mustard seed which in due time grows and flourishes until the birds of the air can make nests in its branches (i.e., Matthew 13:31-32). It would be ever so nice if the risks and sacrifices of a new situation could be comparable to giving up a well-established shade tree for something no worse than a promising young tree with roots wrapped in a big burlap ball. However, we may be confronted instead with the extreme uncertainty of a new God-given opportunity which is comparable to holding only a tiny seed in our hands. To God we indeed may cry out in astonishment, "You've got to be kidding!" as we stare at this tiny seed and we are challenged to believe that what we have in our hands is the tiny beginning of something worth waiting for and something worth working for. It may not be easy to decide whether a job promotion with increased responsibility definitely will allow more time to spend with the family after all the hard work of the start-up phase has been completed. It may not be easy for a church to decide whether remaining in an old declining neighborhood with new patterns of community outreach will help to counteract declining membership and financial support. Like Jacob, we often have to learn the hard way. But with God's grace we can learn what is truly worth waiting for and worth working for, trusting that through God's grace sooner or later even a puny little seed will become a magnificent, tall tree. Like Jacob, we really don't deserve to have God put anything in our hands, even a small seed. But we can rejoice that our gracious God has never left us empty handed, even if it may take many growing pains before we finally obtain the precious prize of something truly worth waiting for and worth working for.

**Proper 13
Pentecost 11
Ordinary Time 18
Genesis 32:22-31**

An Honest And Painful Wrestling Match

Jacob's wrestling match at Peniel is much different from the wrestling matches we see on television today. We become extremely skeptical whenever the wrestling match shows one wrestler flat on the mat allowing his opponent to jump and kick and put on a violent display of growling and groaning, a big theatrical temper tantrum which definitely delights the howling crowd watching this "one ring circus." But rather than yell out, "Fake! Fake!" it's much easier simply to grab the remote control and switch quickly to another channel. Unlike the television wrestling match which we suspect is just a crowd pleaser, one big fake from beginning to end, Jacob's wrestling match is an honest, earnest, all-out struggle with no observers at the scene whatsoever. Neither can we find any comparison between Jacob's wrestling match and the authorized sport of wrestling at the high school and college level where the objective is not to inflict pain but to use a variety of authorized holds and maneuvers to pin the opponent's shoulders to the mat. Unlike high school or college wrestling matches, the main objective of Jacob's wrestling match was to teach Jacob a painful lesson in a big free-for-all scuffle with no official referee to take charge and declare a winner and no restricted repertoire of authorized holds and maneuvers.

The story of Jacob's wrestling match is a story of how Jacob became a better man through his strenuous all-night struggle which taught Jacob a painful lesson of what God expected of him. Jacob is on his way home after many years working for his uncle Laban, and Jacob has gotten word that his brother Esau is coming to meet him with a host of 400 men. This really terrifies Jacob, because it sounds as if Esau is out to get revenge for all the dirty deals that Jacob got away with in depriving Esau of both his birthright and also the deathbed blessing of Isaac, their father. After sending his wives, children, servants, and a whopping present of goats, sheep, camels, cattle, and donkeys on ahead of him to Esau, Jacob is all alone beside the Jabbok River. There we are told that a man wrestles with Jacob until daybreak, and Jacob ends up with a lame hip and new name, Israel. His descendants will be identified hereafter as the people of Israel.

Most of us at a certain age have enough problems with stiff limbs and creaky joints that we would not want to take part in an actual wrestling match, either the big grunt and groan circus we see on television or the authorized gymnasium sport in which two highly skilled athletes become human pretzels in every shape conceivable. But most of us know what it is to have a sleepless night in which we constantly toss and turn and struggle to come to terms with ourselves and with God. We know the kind of wrestling match that is truly a painful experience, for example, when someone is up all night struggling with matters such as what to do with a marriage that has gone from bad to worse, what to say to someone whose feelings have been hurt by cruel and unkind words, how to handle the frightening news of a cancer diagnosis, how to find the courage to speak up and take a stand, regardless of what your friends and neighbors will think. And like Jacob, we too can experience a terrible struggle when God insists upon picking a fight with us and insists that we take part in a wrestling match, because God wants to bring out the best in us, even when we are content in life to take the easy way out and avoid the challenges God would set before us. Whoever put together the story of Jacob's wrestling match in the Old Testament wanted to make it clear that it was to Jacob's credit that he did not back away from wrestling with the mysterious man who actually happened to be God present and active in the form of a human being. Jacob was determined to hang in there and gain some kind of benefit or blessing from his struggle. He says to his adversary, "I will not let you go, unless you bless me" (Genesis 33:26b).

Like Jacob, we are called by God to hang in there when God picks a fight with us and asks us to wrestle with the truth of ourselves and the truth of God. Whenever God wants to wrestle with us, God's challenge is very much the same regardless of whether we are wrestling with the terrible truth of a bad marriage, the terrible truth of unkind and cruel words that have hurt someone, the terrible truth of a cancer diagnosis, the terrible truth of an unpopular, costly stand to take for the sake of justice and fair play, or the terrible truth of how we would do almost anything to avoid God's challenge to bring out the best of us. Regardless of what it is we are up against, we are called by God and we are challenged by God to hang in there and hang in there and hang in there, wrestling with all our heart and mind and strength, until finally God blesses us with whatever it takes for us to walk forward as the kind of person God wants us to be in the direction God wants us to go.

Jacob's new name, Israel, is given to him to indicate that he has been in a wrestling match in which he has prevailed and has come out of this experience a better man. The name Israel has a double meaning. The name can mean "God strives" and it also can mean "the one who strives with God." Jacob strives with God and Jacob prevails — not in the sense of defeating God, but in the sense that Jacob's life is preserved and not destroyed as a result of this wrestling match that left Jacob with considerable pain. As Jacob describes his painful, soul-searching experience, "... I have seen God face to face, and yet my life is preserved" (Genesis 32:30). This is not the proud boast of Jacob, the cocky, clever wheeler-dealer. This is the humble confession of a man who through severe growing pains has begun to change from Jacob the rascal to Jacob the righteous one. In many ways Jacob is still the same old Jacob who still has a lot to learn the hard way. But the wrestling match helps to make him a much better man in that it strengthens his confidence and his determination to deal steadfastly with life's most stubborn problems. It increases his desire to maintain a closer relationship with God, regardless of how difficult or complex Jacob's life may be. Jacob's wrestling match with God left him feeling deeply grateful that he had actually survived after confronting God in the dark hours of the night face to face. In the book of Exodus God says to Moses, "You cannot see my face; for no one shall see me and live" (Exodus 33:20). It was absolutely essential that the face-to-face wrestling match between God and Jacob took place at night, that God stopped the wrestling match before daybreak so that Jacob could not see God's face fully and clearly in the light of day. Jacob realized that he was lucky to be alive and did not end up a dead man from his face-to-face encounter with God, thanks to the nighttime hours' protective cover of darkness. And Jacob, therefore, named the place of the wrestling match, Peniel, which means in Hebrew "the face of God."

Now this painful experience is by no means the last of all the many experiences of spiritual growth that Jacob still must go through in order to become a much better man than the clever rascal he has always been. But when Jacob finally meets Esau, it becomes obvious that Jacob has begun to be a better man as a result of his painful wrestling match. Esau welcomes Jacob with forgiveness and with open arms and does not want Jacob to give him the huge present of so many valuable animals — goats, sheep, camels, cattle, and donkeys. But Jacob begs him to "... accept my present from my hand; for truly to see your face is like seeing the face of God — since you have received me with such favor. Please accept my gift, because God has dealt graciously with me ..." (Genesis 33:10-11). Yes, Jacob can be reconciled to his brother, Esau, and make peace with him, because God has dealt graciously with Jacob, allowing Jacob to see God's face and survive. God allowed Jacob to see his brother's face radiantly reflecting the God-like spirit of peace and forgiveness instead of the bitter spirit of anger and retaliation.

Have you ever wished you could change your name? There are people who for one reason or another obviously did not want to be called by the original name their parents gave them. John Edgar Hoover became better known as J. Edgar Hoover, founder of the FBI, and Norma Jean Baker became famous as Marilyn Monroe. Today there are a lot of hyphenated last names that are created, for example, when Mr. Johnson and Miss Bancroft want to get married and be known thereafter as Mr. and Mrs. Bancroft-Johnson in order to do justice to what they feel is their true identity as a married couple. It is never a small matter when someone changes his or her name for one reason or another. And it was no small matter for Jacob to be given the new name, Israel. The name Jacob was derived from the event of the birth of the twins, Jacob and Esau. Esau was born first, but Jacob was born with his hand grasping the heel of Esau, an early sign that he would take advantage of his older brother and try to take Esau's place as the head of the family. The name Jacob comes from Hebrew that can mean "to seize by the heel" or "he overreaches." Jacob certainly lived up to his name in his clever efforts to seize the heel of every opportunity and overreach well beyond the limits of what he was properly entitled to as the youngest of the twins.

We know how a name or a nickname definitely can make a difference in how someone develops a sense of self-identity. If someone is known as Stonewall Jackson or Calamity Jane, we would expect this person to be a tough customer to deal with. As the first black woman in the nineteenth century traveling far and wide to speak out publicly against the evils of slavery, Isabella Baumfree took on the name Sojourner Truth. Since a sojourner is someone who stays in a place only temporarily before moving on, this courageous woman, Sojourner Truth, lived up to her name as a person continually on the move to declare the truth about the cause to abolish slavery. It was no small matter for Jacob to receive a new name, Israel. Instead of picturing himself as Jacob, one who cleverly seizes the heel of every opportunity, Jacob now had to begin living up to the picture of himself as Israel, one who had wrestled with God and who had prevailed and survived as a better man for the experience. The name Israel, with its double meaning "God strives" or "one who strives with God," had double implications for the people of Israel. On one hand, the name Israel was a reminder that God would continue to strive with his chosen people and hang in there and wrestle with them in order to bring out the best in them. On the other hand, the name Israel served to indicate that God's chosen people would continue to strive with God and to hang in there and to wrestle with the stubborn issues and demands of what God expected with them. The relationship between God and Israel would continue to be a strenuous wrestling match with many growing pains and nothing easy or simple.

Looking at the history of Jacob and his descendants, each of us needs to ask ourselves, "Will I be remembered in years to come by my family and others who look up to me as someone who hangs in there, someone who does not back off from wrestling with the truth of myself, the truth of my life, the truth of my God?" Yes, there are times when our prayer life may be as peaceful as the lift we get when we lie flat on our backs on a beautiful day at the beach with our eyes closed, listening to the cries of the sea gulls and the thunderous pounding of the waves. But it would be a mistake to think that prayer time spent with God is intended always to be like an awe-inspiring, breath-taking mountaintop view of the magnificent, snow-covered Swiss Alps, an exhilarating John Denver outdoor sensation of "Rocky Mountain High."[1] Any misery-afflicted drug addict or alcoholic can tell you there is no foolproof or guaranteed way to get high or stay high. Sometimes our prayer life is an honest and painful wrestling match that knocks us down from life's lofty heights, slams us down to the ground, and brings us face to face with the God who loves us enough to pick a fight with us. Even for Jesus, prayer at times became a painful wrestling match, such as the showdown between Jesus and the temptations of Satan out in the hot, dry wilderness or the agonizing struggle Jesus went through in the Garden of Gethsemane. When prayer for us becomes a really intense struggle, the payoff for hanging in there is a precious heritage of spiritual growing pains and spiritual endurance, a spiritual heritage that is truly worth passing along to all those who might want to look up to us as a worthy example and role model to follow whenever the narrow, winding road of faith is mighty tough to travel. What better heritage can you or I pass on to our children, our family, and others who look up to us than to be remembered in years to come as someone who hangs in there and hangs in there and hangs in there, someone who does not back off from wrestling with "the truth of myself, the truth of my life, the truth of my God"?

---

1. John Denver and Michael Taylor, "Rocky Mountain High," Cherry Lane Music Publishing Company, Inc., 1972.

**Proper 14
Pentecost 12
Ordinary Time 19
Genesis 37:1-4, 12-28**

When Life Is The Pits!

Joseph got thrown in a big hole by his brothers, and he quickly discovered what life is like down in the pits. He was the favorite of his father Jacob, and this just didn't sit too well with the other boys. It certainly didn't help much that Joseph had such a big mouth and had actually told his brothers all about his glorious dream in which Joseph was the big honcho out in the wheat fields at harvest time. In this dream Joseph had a big, beautiful bundle of wheat before which his brothers' sheaves of wheat were humiliated and forced to bow down. Even Jacob didn't like one of the dreams Joseph had when Joseph bragged how the sun, the moon, and eleven stars bowed down to him We really can't help but second-guess Jacob for being so foolish as to put his young son up on a pedestal wearing a fancy, razzle-dazzle, long-sleeved coat that certainly outdazzled any ordinary work clothes for tending herds that Joseph's older brothers had to wear. Anyway, Joseph's life is suddenly changed from life at the top of the heap to life down in the pits, and he ends up being sold as a slave to a traveling caravan on its way to Egypt.

Indeed, life can be the pits where you end up way down at the bottom, if somebody doesn't like you one bit and if somebody is extremely jealous of your personal advantages and your place in the sun. Unfortunately, this can happen to you, regardless of whether or not you have had sense enough to keep your mouth shut and not crow like a rooster to advertise how great you are. Some painful and horrible examples of this are the terrorist bombings of the American embassies that took place in Kenya and Tanzania. If you are an American traveling overseas or if you are an American embassy staff person or an American military man or woman stationed in certain parts of the world, you had better be aware that there are those who just plain don't like Americans and who are just waiting for the chance, through kidnapping or terrorist attacks, to make life for Americans the absolute, dreadful pits. If a college football team is rated number one in the country, you can expect every opponent to be fired up to try to beat this team. The quarterback can expect the opponent's defense to do everything possible to sack the quarterback and inflict as much physical punishment as the rules permit. Life for a star quarterback in the National Football League can be the pits when you are getting blitzed and hammered to the ground again and again by your opponent who is out to get you. Certainly the story of Joseph's trials and troubles might provide a very handy excuse for every underachiever whose motto in life is, "Keep your mouth shut and don't ever make waves and you won't get hurt."

Perhaps a defense lawyer for Joseph could try to win sympathy from a tough-minded, modern day jury who might feel that, yes, life in the pits is truly awful, but Joseph was a big-mouthed brat who got exactly what he deserved. Joseph's attorney could point out that the world today has plenty of cocky, conceited kids who simply are not mature enough to handle all the enormous attention which they get just because some eager beaver parents are determined to push these immature kids into the very center of the stage with a high beam spotlight directly overhead. The loud-mouthed child on the Little League team often has a loud-mouthed parent who drives everyone absolutely nuts by bragging non-stop about what a hot shot super star little Junior certainly is. So in Joseph's defense, his attorney could argue to the jury that little Joseph never asked to be his proud papa's favorite son; that was Jacob's not-so-bright idea! Also, in Joseph's defense, we need to realize that the story of young Joseph's dreams of future greatness was intended in the Old Testament to serve as an early prediction of Joseph's God-given destiny to become someone very different from the other boys, someone who in later years would make all the difference between life or death for Jacob and Joseph's brothers. So although Joseph certainly would have done well to avoid bragging and boasting, a shrewd defense attorney could argue that it wasn't at all Joseph's fault that he had powerful dreams of future greatness. Indeed, these dreams were authentic signs of God's great plan for Joseph's life in years to come. Certainly such powerful dreams were an awful lot to expect a young lad to handle in a tactful manner without crowing like a proud rooster. Regardless of a defense attorney's arguments to win sympathy for Joseph, a jury still might find it extremely hard to overlook the fact that Joseph definitely has to accept his share of responsibility for his sorry predicament that he ended up down in a big pit and was sold into slavery. Although God definitely has great plans for Joseph, God also intends for Joseph to go through some very intense growing pains, so that Joseph will be ready for the role God wants him to play in the history of his people.

God's justice affects not only Joseph but also Jacob and Joseph's brothers. Jacob's grief over the favorite son he presumes to be dead is understood in the Old Testament as one more way in which Jacob is being punished for his crafty misdeeds years ago when he was the favorite son of his mother Rebekah, and when he took unfair advantage of Esau, his brother. Joseph's brothers in later years will experience much God-given grief when a famine in their homeland forces them to go to Egypt where they are forced to face up to the painful truth of how they had mistreated Joseph. For the time being, the brothers of Joseph are able to use the blood-stained clothes of Joseph in order to prevent Jacob from knowing the terrible truth of what happened to Joseph. But Joseph's growing pains, Jacob's grief, and Joseph's brothers' desperate, emergency survival trip to Egypt are all part of God's plan to see that justice is done and that a painful lesson is learned by all concerned.

Perhaps Joseph's brothers could hire a defense lawyer to try to appease a jury which is totally horrified or furious that young Joseph would receive such harsh treatment from his older siblings. The defense could try to win sympathy by pointing out that at least one of the brothers stepped in to stop Joseph from being put to death. The only problem with that approach is that the Old Testament story can't seem to agree as to which brother should be credited with preventing bloodshed. On one hand, the story says that it was Reuben who stepped in to suggest that Joseph be thrown into the pit alive, because Reuben intended later on to get Joseph out of the pit and take him back to Jacob. But then the story says that it was Judah, another brother, who prevented bloodshed by suggesting that instead of killing Joseph, the brothers should sell him to a traveling caravan of Ishmaelites on their way to Egypt. The story becomes confusing in that we really don't know whether to give credit to Reuben or to Judah that Joseph's life was spared. We also don't know whether it was a caravan of Ishmaelites or a caravan of Midianites that took Joseph to Egypt. So a skeptical modern day jury might say to the brothers' defense lawyer, "Hey, how come you can't get all your facts straight in trying to show grounds for mercy toward these brothers, since first you say it was Reuben and then you say it was Judah who was the merciful brother, and then you change your story completely regarding whose caravan was involved in taking Joseph to Egypt?" Fortunately the fate of Jacob and Joseph and Joseph's brothers was in the hands of God and not in the hands of a modern-day jury!

To get a deeper appreciation of Jacob's trials and tribulations as a father who believes his favorite son has been killed, let us try to picture a complicated situation where life at its worst is really the pits, a really terrible predicament. To make matters worse, if we were to try to discover the whole truth of the situation, we would find that nobody can provide a reliable story we can count upon to be true, a story with no contradictions and no inconsistencies regarding what has actually happened. For example, let's suppose you are a modern day Jacob. You're told that your son, little Joe, has been killed in an auto accident, as evidenced by bloody clothes found by the side of the road. But there are witnesses to the accident who, for one reason or another, fail to tell you that your son is still alive and an ambulance took the youngster to a hospital. However, if you ever got a report from these witnesses, you really might wonder if this is a likely story. Nobody agrees as to who actually took action to save the day or which emergency squad actually showed up to take little Joe to some unknown destination.

This might sound like a far-fetched nightmare with no resemblance to reality, but think of a situation where a family gets separated during a flood or a fire. In trying to locate a missing child, a parent receives clothing that seems like evidence of the child's death but then gets conflicting rumors of how the child's life was spared and what was the final outcome. How often did African-American slaves have to live with the torment of conflicting, inconsistent evidence whether or not a family member had died or was still alive or had been sold to another slaveholder? This torment would be even more unbearable if the family first believed their loved one was dead, but then they began receiving conflicting, unconfirmed stories of how a family member's life had been spared or how someone had actually transported this person to an unknown slave owner.

Nobody told the truth to Jacob about what had happened to Joseph out in the fields. Jacob's grief over Joseph was never relieved until many years later after his sons came back from Egypt to tell him that Joseph was alive. In many ways life was indeed the pits for Jacob who never got over the terrible news that his son was dead. There was no way Jacob's agony would be relieved in a relatively short time like the typical triumphant conclusion of a one-night television drama just prior to the eleven o'clock news. What makes life in the pits really the pits is that there is usually no quick and simple solution that makes everything suddenly turn out okay. Joseph didn't spend forever down in the deep hole, but the long caravan ride to Egypt must have seemed like forever and ever to him. The boy Joseph probably had extreme fear and dread and uncertainty as to what being a slave in Egypt would be like, similar to the fear and terror of the African captives crammed into tight quarters below the top deck of a slave ship headed across the sea for a distant destination strange and unfamiliar. When life is really the pits and what lies ahead is uncertain, unknown, and truly terrifying, it's not easy to hang in there and believe that God is doing everything possible.

And yet the story of Joseph's rescue from a deep hole is a story telling how God can be trusted to come through for us when life is truly the pits. Think of all the people gathered here in this congregation today, and you are bound to think of someone you know here today who can tell you from firsthand experience that when life was just plain awful God was right there with comfort and strength. Whenever the people of the church reach out to show loving concern and lend a helping hand to people for whom life is truly the pits, this can be the most convincing evidence to people who are down in the depths of deepest despair that there indeed is a God who never abandons us. But there are times when it is not easy for you and me to stand alongside those who are really down in the pits, such as someone in constant pain which no medicine can eliminate, or someone whose child has been missing for days or weeks after being kidnapped by a stranger. Indeed, it can be downright scary and overwhelming for us to hang tough, hang on, and hang in there, giving love and encouragement.

But God is always ready and able to give us, somehow, the strength and the courage it takes for us to provide loving care and steady support to people who are down in the pits, whether it is someone whose marriage has suddenly and unexpectedly disintegrated or someone whose medical examination and x-rays have produced unexpected and discouraging news. God is never absent or far away even in those times when worse comes to worst with no escape possible from a terminal illness or an airplane crash or a car bomb set off by terrorists. The death and resurrection of Jesus give us strong reassurance that God will never, never abandon his faithful people even when eternal life is God's only remaining alternative for those who are trapped down in a terrible dead end pit with absolutely no way out. Yes, there are times when Murphy's Law may seem stronger than God's law and life is really the pits. But we can give thanks and praise to the great God who raised up Joseph from a deep hole, who lifted Jesus up from the grave, and who will rescue us again and again from the depths of death and despair both now and at the end of our earthly journey, the God who will never, never abandon us to life forever down in the pits.

**Proper 15
Pentecost 13
Ordinary Time 20
Genesis 45:1-15**

When It Hurts To Forgive

How could Joseph possibly forgive his brothers after all they did to him? He actually says to his brothers, "Do not be distressed or angry with yourselves, because you sold me here; for God sent me before you to preserve life" (Genesis 45:5). Forgiveness for most people doesn't come easy. There is plenty of evidence that many people find it absolutely impossible to forgive those who have done something absolutely terrible. We live in an age when violence and cruelty make the front page of the newspaper again and again. A murderer is sentenced to death for a horrible crime in which the victim experienced a most terrifying, heartless death. The victim's family rejoices that the murderer has received the death penalty, and members of the family insist that they definitely want to be on hand to witness the execution and see the killer get what he deserves. A police officer is shot and left paralyzed, unable to continue his career or support his family. Should his heartbroken spouse be expected to forgive whoever pulled the trigger? A child is physically or sexually abused by a close relative, and the trauma of that terrible experience leaves emotional scars which even the most skillful psychotherapy can never completely remove. Should that child be expected as a child or in later years as an adult to forgive whoever made that child's life a living nightmare? Joseph as a young boy experienced the terrible nightmare of being thrown into a deep pit by his older brothers. Certainly he knew the extreme terror of realizing that his brothers were considering putting him to death, before they finally decided to sell him into slavery and ship him off to Egypt. Should Joseph as a man be expected to forgive his brothers for the cruel nightmare they put him through? Could Joseph now really say to his brothers, "Everything is okay, boys! My coming to Egypt was God's plan for my life, and so I don't hold it against you at all for what you did to me"?

Our Old Testament lesson from chapter 45 of Genesis, the story of Joseph forgiving his brothers, becomes much more believable after we find out what has happened earlier to Joseph and his brothers in chapters 42, 43, and 44. When we read what happens in these earlier chapters, we will come to understand that Joseph is no extraordinary person for whom forgiveness comes easy. Indeed, Joseph is very much like the average person for whom it is very hard to forgive those who have made someone's life absolutely awful. In no way is it easy for Joseph to forgive his brothers! Chapter 42 tells us there is a shortage of food due to a severe famine, and Joseph's brothers show up in Egypt looking to buy grain to take back to their homeland. They do not recognize Joseph, but Joseph definitely recognizes them. Yet he does not let the brothers know this. Instead he treats them like total strangers and speaks harshly to them. He accuses them of being spies with evil intent. He has them put in jail for three days. Then he tells them to go home after leaving one brother, Simeon, behind in Egypt as a hostage. He tells them to take grain with them but to return again to Egypt with their youngest brother, Benjamin, who had not made the trip with them.

In chapter 42 we find that Joseph definitely is hard-nosed and hard-boiled when he has the shock of his life — an unexpected reunion with the brothers who had sold him into slavery. Yet Joseph is not able to be completely stern and severe in how he handles the situation. We are told that he has to withdraw from the scene and break down and cry. We are told that he gives orders for the brothers' sacks to be filled with grain and he sees to it that their money that they have paid for the grain is returned secretly and placed in the grain sacks. He makes sure that provisions for the return trip are given to the brothers, so that they can travel back home with ample food and supplies for the journey. Then in chapter 43 the brothers return to Egypt; this time Benjamin is with them. Again Joseph has his moments of anguish when he must withdraw from his brothers in order to break down and cry. But although Joseph has seen signs that his brothers are sorry for what they did to Joseph years ago, Joseph takes steps to put his brothers to a further test. After all, were they really sorry for what they had done to him, or was this show of humility and remorse simply a big crybaby act to win sympathy and increase the brothers' chances of being given food to take back home?

In chapter 44 the brothers once again have full sacks of grain for the journey home, but, unknown to them, Joseph's silver cup has been placed secretly in Benjamin's sack. Joseph lets the brothers travel a short distance; then Joseph's steward is sent to accuse the brothers of stealing the silver cup and to give the order that Benjamin must be detained in Egypt. The brothers then return quickly to Joseph. One brother, Judah, pleads frantically with Joseph to please, please allow Benjamin to return with them, because their father Jacob will surely suffer and die from grief if Benjamin does not return. All this sets the stage for chapter 45 where Joseph simply cannot stand it any longer. After he breaks down and cries, he finally makes it known to his brothers who he is. In spite of his intense anger and resentment regarding things that have happened in the past, Joseph greatly needs to be reconciled and reunited with his family. Joseph realizes that God has indeed placed him in a position to save his family from starvation. Finally Joseph forgives!

We can well imagine Joseph's being torn apart by a wide range of emotions. He very likely would be overwhelmed at times by deep resentment and harsh anger toward his brothers for the way they had treated them. Yet Joseph also certainly realized that as a young boy his big mouth and his glorious dreams of future greatness had only served to make his brothers deeply resentful toward him. Joseph has a very strong desire to see his father Jacob once again, as well as a strong feeling of affection for Benjamin, the youngest brother closest in age to Joseph. Any bitter desire on Joseph's part to get even or get revenge is in a sharp tug of war conflict with Joseph's coming to realize that God has placed him in a powerful position to offer his family a new lease on life.

A tremendous tug of war rages out of control within Joseph until finally he feels compelled to reveal himself to his brothers and forgive them. Real forgiveness never comes about easily whenever there is a vicious and violent war involving feelings of deep hurt or agonizing doubts whether to believe that words of remorse and regret are sincere. For example, in a marriage in which one partner has had an affair outside the marriage but then expresses deep remorse and asks to be forgiven, there are apt to be intense feelings regarding whether or not forgiveness should and can be given, whether or not to take the risk of believing that remorse is sincere. George Wallace, former governor of Alabama, in his later years expressed deep regret for his views and his actions in support of racial segregation, and he asked many times to be forgiven. But some were extremely skeptical as to whether Wallace was sincere in his desire for forgiveness or whether he was simply out to win votes from black people in one more try to be re-elected to office.[1] Yet others, including Jesse Jackson and Coretta Scott King, were willing to forgive him and take him at his word when George Wallace said again and again, "I was wrong."[2] In the television movie production *George Wallace*, there is the powerful scene where Wallace, paralyzed from being shot and helpless in a wheel chair, painfully acknowledges his guilt before the congregation of the Dexter Avenue Baptist Church and asks them to forgive him. We see the slow and gradual change in the congregation's attitude from cool and suspicious skepticism to a glad and warm willingness to shake Wallace's hand and wish him well.[3] Forgiveness is for real when forgiveness doesn't come easy but involves anguish on the part of those who offer forgiveness.

Have you ever been in a situation like that of Joseph? Have you ever been in a situation where no matter how badly you had been treated by someone, you became aware that you still were in a powerful position to make something good happen for this person? Furthermore, you would have to be the person who took the first step to bridge the broken relationship with someone who perhaps had made an all-out effort to humiliate you or make you miserable. Parents often find themselves in this type of situation in relating to their children. When your child has done something that hurts your feelings, whether it's a young child who rudely tries to embarrass you in front of your friends or a teenager who tells you to get lost, go fly a kite, or something even worse in x-rated language, usually it's still up to you to use your parental power to make something positive happen and to take the first step to bridge the broken relationship. Even when the child or the teenager is sorry for what has been said or done, it still may be largely up to you to use your parental power to take the initiative in picking up the pieces. It finally became painfully obvious to Joseph that it was time for him to accept his brothers' expressions of remorse and put away his anger, using his power as an Egyptian administrator to make positive things happen for his family. Joseph tells his brothers to go back home and tell Jacob, "Thus says your son, Joseph: God has made me lord of all Egypt; come down to me, do not delay. You shall settle in the land of Goshen, and you shall be near me, you and your children and your children's children, as well as your flocks, your herds, and all that you have. I will provide for you there — since there are five more years of famine to come — so that you and your household, and all that you have, will not come to poverty" (Genesis 45:9-11). Because Joseph took the first painful step to mend the shattered relationship between himself and his family, the people of Israel were given refuge in Egypt as a way to thrive and survive as the people God had chosen for a great purpose.

    A broken or bitter relationship can continue for years and years, until finally somebody is willing to take the first step to mend the relationship. Only in recent years have Protestants and Catholics in Northern Ireland been willing to take any initial steps toward peaceful reconciliation to end the terrible suffering caused by many years of bloody conflict. The reconciliation between Joseph and his brothers was a two-way street in which after Joseph took the difficult first step, Joseph and his brothers were able then to begin to reach out to each other to rebuild trust and to bridge the gap. Complete and full reconciliation doesn't happen for Joseph and his brothers until much later, as recorded in the last chapter of the book of Genesis. But at least in Egypt the painful first steps had been taken. Forgiveness is most effective when it hurts to forgive and when it hurts to be forgiven. Joseph experienced the pain of offering forgiveness, but his brothers experienced the pain of being forgiven, the pain of realizing that the young boy they had cruelly thrown into the deep pit years ago was now the grown-up man who graciously and generously had rescued them from starvation and kept them from falling into the deep hole of hopeless despair.

God's forgiveness is never intended to let a murderer get away with murder and escape the pain of facing up to the terrible facts of the crime that has been committed. When Jesus forgave those who crucified him, the execution squad did not escape from experiencing the terrible pain of what they had done. The dreadful day that Jesus died concluded with a terrifying earthquake and other events so earthshaking and terrifying that the Roman soldiers stared in utter horror and amazement at the man on the cross who, unlike most crucified victims, did not swear and curse at his tormenters. And the execution squad cried out, "Truly this man was God's Son" (Matthew 27:54)! Both the story of Joseph and the story of the crucified Christ show that God's forgiveness is not an expedient, "quickie" pain killer that prevents us from facing up to the terrible truth of who we are at our very worst, or facing up to the humbling, heartbreaking truth of what it dearly costs God and what it takes for God to bring out the very best in us. God's forgiveness makes it possible for us sinners to receive a new lease on life, but there is no painkilling anesthesia to ease the delivery process of our rebirth. New life through God's forgiveness is never without its necessary labor pains or its many growing pains.

---

1. Cf., Stephan Lesher, *George Wallace: American Populist* (New York: Addison-Wesley Publishing Company, 1994), p. 501.

2. Cf., *ibid.*, pp. 503-504.

3. Cf., John Frankenheimer, producer and director, *George Wallace*, television motion picture, TNT, 1997.

**Proper 16
Pentecost 14
Ordinary Time 21
Exodus 1:8—2:10**

Nothing Left But
A Baby In A Basket

Every head of a family would like to do everything possible to make life better for the next generation: the children of the family and also the grandchildren. For example, a lot of time and money goes into the writing up of a will or a trust agreement whereby one generation's financial assets, property, and personal belongings will be passed along to the next generation in a manner designed to reduce estate taxes and to guarantee that the next generation receives the maximum financial benefit. Joseph, son of Jacob, wanted to guarantee a secure future for his family. He had become one of ancient Egypt's most powerful government officials. He had saved his family from starvation and had used his influence to give them refuge in Egypt. There was nothing more he could do to make things better for his family and their offspring. And as long as Joseph was alive (and the Bible says he lived to be 110 years old!), life was very good for the people of Israel who were living in a foreign land. But in spite of the best plans and preparations, there is no way the head of a family can guarantee complete safety and security for the next generation of children and grandchildren. This becomes extremely obvious after this person's death, especially if there is absolutely nobody around in a position of influence who knew the head of the family very well and who, for the sake of a longtime friendship, would try to assist the surviving family in critical, important matters not covered by any will or trust agreement or legal rights. After Joseph died, a new king arose in Egypt who did not know Joseph and who felt he was in no way obligated to honor whatever agreements Joseph had made to give the people of Israel a new lease on life as alien residents in a foreign land. Under the new king the Israelites were now referred to as "Hebrews" or *hapiru*, a term in the ancient Near East that refers to any group of marginal people who have no social standing, own no land, and are considered "low class folks" who are excluded and despised.

Down in Egypt Jacob's descendants, the Hebrews, had Pharoah, the new king of Egypt, really worried. The numbers of the Hebrew people had increased so rapidly that Pharoah was afraid they would soon have enough numbers and strength to rise up and leave the country, depriving the king of available cheap labor. So he tried to reduce their vigor and their numbers by submitting the Hebrews to hard labor in extremely harsh conditions, but this just didn't work at all. The Egyptians kept piling on the workload and making working conditions as mean and miserable as possible. But the Hebrews kept increasing in numbers and vitality. Pharoah in frantic desperation then told the Hebrew midwives to kill all the newborn Hebrew boys but to let the girls live. But the midwives let the boys live, and when Pharoah asked "How come you let this happen?" Pharoah was dumb enough to believe the midwives' shrewd explanation that the boy babies were being born faster than the midwives could arrive on the scene. Anyway, the people of Israel under God's blessing continued to multiply in numbers and in strength, while working conditions under the Egyptians continued to get worse. Working with mortar and bricks out in the hot sun was really awful.

How often it is that regardless of how carefully one generation tries to make things better for the next generation, it still remains for someone in a later generation to rise up and save the day. Joseph was dead. His influence had come to an end. Life on Easy Street for the Israelites had now become a living hell on earth. Things got so bad that there was nothing left to hope for, nothing left but a baby in a basket floating among the reeds along the river bank, nothing left for the people of Israel except years and years of sweat and suffering until this baby Moses could grow up and become the leader appointed by God to rise up and save the day for the people of Israel. So what happens to a people in captivity when there is nothing left but a baby in a basket? How does God provide for God's chosen people during the many years that must pass by until this baby is the grown man who will rise up and save the day for God's chosen people?

Our scripture lesson today shows us at least three ways in which God enables faithful people to hang tough, hang on, and hang in there when life is at its very worst. First of all, in spite of the Egyptians' efforts to reduce the numbers of the Hebrew people through hard labor, the chosen people through the grace of God continued to multiply in numbers. It has been true throughout history that persecution of God's chosen people only leads to an increase in their numbers. The Romans persecuted the Christians, often forcing them to die for their faith in the arena where wild beasts and a bloodthirsty crowd had the upper hand, but the Christians increased in numbers and eventually Christianity became the official religion of the Roman empire. The church continues to hang tough and survive today in China, Guatamela, and other areas of the world where church leaders and church members have been imprisoned or tortured or murdered because of their faith. Again and again God enables God's chosen people to increase in physical numbers and spiritual strength, to hang tough, hang on, and hang in there throughout the very worst that can happen.

Secondly, God gives God's chosen people shrewd instincts for how to cope with the forces of evil in order to survive within an evil system. Pharoah asks the Hebrew midwives, Shiprah and Puah, why the Hebrew boy babies were allowed to live, in spite of his strict orders to have all Hebrew boy babies put to death. And the midwives reply, "Because the Hebrew women are not like the Egyptian women; for they are vigorous and give birth before the midwife comes to them" (Exodus 1:19). Because the midwives feared God and kept the faith, God gave them shrewd instincts for how to respond to Pharoah's orders. The arrogant Pharoah was dumb enough to believe what the midwives told him. Those who are at the top of the heap sometimes end up completely underestimating the resourcefulness of those who are considered to be at the bottom of the barrel. Many white American plantation owners promoted the teaching of the Christian religion to their black slaves, because the plantation owners thought that sound religious instruction would produce slaves who were more docile and obedient. However, black slaves found increased inner strength through their Christian faith, and the white slave owners had absolutely no idea how the singing of spirituals gave expression and encouragement to the slaves' longing for freedom. James Cone, black theologian, tells us that just as God delivered the Israelites from Egyptian slavery by drowning Pharoah's army in the sea, black slaves believed God also would deliver them from American slavery, as expressed in the spiritual: "Oh, Mary, don't you weep, don't you moan, Oh, Mary, don't you weep, don't you moan, Pharoah's army got drownded, Oh, Mary, don't you weep."[1] The religion that was supposed to transform black slaves into docile, obedient servants of their white masters ended up transforming black slaves into shrewd, faithful servants of God. Spirituals often contained secret messages. Singing "Steal away to Jesus" could be a special signal to tell the congregation that a secret slave meeting would be held in the woods.[2]

A third way in which God acted in behalf of God's chosen people was to make the oppressive system yield unexpected benefits for those who were oppressed by this system. Pharoah's daughter obviously disagreed with her father's decree to have all the Hebrew boy babies killed. Moses' sister, Miriam, was shrewd enough to obtain Moses' mother to care for him in behalf of the Egyptian princess who adopted the baby Moses, made him a "prince of Egypt,"[3] and gave him as a child all the advantages of Egyptian culture. As a result Moses acquired the education and the leadership capabilities that would enable him someday to rise up and save the day for God's chosen people. In a similar way, Mahatma Gandhi's study of law in London and Nelson Mandela's study of law in Johannesburg strengthened their capabilities to be leaders in their struggles against oppression in India and South Africa. The rescue of the baby in the basket from the waters of the river by the Egyptian princess is ironically a sign pointing toward something greater that lies ahead, the rescue of the people of Israel through the waters of the sea led by Moses, the well educated, highly capable "prince of Egypt." In our Old Testament story about the baby Moses the Hebrew word for basket, *teba*, is the same word used for Noah's ark in the Old Testament story of the great flood that covered the earth. The baby's basket, his *teba*, is his "ark" floating safely on the waters of the river. This tiny, waterproof basket becomes eventually for Israel an encouraging reminder of the ark that saved Noah and his family from the great flood. The baby's basket floating on the water becomes a symbol of God's power to save the chosen people from the deepest waters of death and despair.

At one time or another just about everyone is up against some form of oppression in which someone is deliberately trying to make us as miserable as possible. Family life can become a state of oppression where women, children, and even elderly relatives are at the mercy of cruel and violent forms of abuse. Sexual harassment in the workplace is extremely humiliating and can be very difficult to stop. Migrant workers may have no choice but to work in fruit orchards or vegetable harvest fields where pesticides and filthy living conditions endanger workers' health. Expensive garments may be made in sweatshop conditions for a miserable level of pay and a threat of reprisal if the worker wants to quit the job. There are high pressure work environments where the supervisor exercises rigid control allowing no negotiation at all regarding "the way we get things done around here."

But there are valuable lessons to be learned from the three ways shown in our scripture lesson how God enables faithful people to hang tough, hang on, and hang in there when life is at its very worst. First of all, if situations in our own lives become truly oppressive and very discouraging, we need to remember that oppression actually can increase the numbers and the determination of those who want to resist oppression. Instead of going it alone in a terribly oppressive situation we need to join hands with those who are in the same boat. Secret hide-away shelters for bruised and battered women enable these women to regain strength and self-esteem by joining hands and sharing their hurts and their hopes with one another. Secondly, when someone exercises control over us in an arrogant way, God can show us shrewd ways to thrive and survive, if we, like the Hebrew midwives, are willing to keep our hearts and our ears open to God. When a work environment is under the authority of an incompetent, domineering supervisor or administrator, a dedicated, competent employee who has managed to survive is very apt to be an employee who has learned shrewd and perhaps justifiable techniques to keep the arrogant boss at a safe distance so that the employee can do the job in a more efficient, effective manner.

Thirdly, whenever it seems "you can't beat the system," we can learn how to make some of the systems of the world work for us in a way that increases our own strength and capability. For example, we all have had our gripes and complaints about computers and computer systems. A sign in an office said, "To err is human. To really foul things up takes a computer." We truly have reason to be concerned how computer systems can violate our privacy by giving others ample access to what is supposed to be confidential, personal information. We don't want the Internet to expose our children to obscene online material. It is alarming how the computer operations essential for military defense, air traffic controllers, hospitals, libraries, or business management can be so extremely vulnerable to computer hackers or computer viruses. But our best defense against the "evils of the computer age" is to learn how to operate a computer, especially if we are going to take advantage of the Internet's most valuable resources. Are we ever too old to learn how to get the many benefits that a home computer can give us? In some communities senior citizens are now getting lessons in computer techniques from teenagers who are eager to help and very proud that they, for once, can show their elders a thing or two. Here is a definite reminder that in our complex world where many problems may never be resolved within our own lifetime, we definitely need to be preparing the younger generation for roles of leadership. Who knows? A baby boy or baby girl we now see in a laundry basket or a crib or a stroller could be a future Moses or a future Miriam who will grow up to play a vital leadership role some day as one of God's chosen people.

1. Cf., James Cone, *The Spirituals And The Blues: An Interpretation* (New York: The Seabury Press, 1972), pp. 23-35.

2. Cf., *ibid.*, p. 90.

3. Brenda Chapman, Steve Hickner, and Simon Wells, directors, *Prince Of Egypt*, animated motion picture, Dreamworks, 1998.

**Proper 17
Pentecost 15
Ordinary Time 22
Exodus 3:1-15**

I Really Am Who I Am!

Have you ever been driving down the road and seen something so irresistible that you ended up going out of your way to take a closer look? Perhaps because you were in a hurry to get somewhere, you at first didn't want to go through the bother of stopping the car and getting out. But stop you did and get out you did. And so you ended up seeing a beautiful waterfall at the end of a short trail. Or you ended up in a gift shop which had a lovely old antique clock, just exactly what would fit in that special corner of the kitchen. Or you ended up at a church service far away from home where the friendly congregation made you feel welcome, and it was an interesting adventure to sing different types of hymns and take part in a worship service very different from your own back home. And after these experiences when you returned to your car from the waterfall or the gift shop or the church at the side of the road, recall how many times you have given thanks and have said to yourself, "And just think! I almost didn't stop!"

We can't know for sure what really happened when Moses turned aside to see a bush that looked like it was on fire. Did the rays of the sun pass through the leaves of this bush in a way that gave the bush a fiery glow? Who knows? What is most important in this story from the Old Testament is that Moses stopped what he was doing and turned aside to see what God wanted him to see. After all, perhaps Moses could have said to himself, "Why bother?" Moses had found a secure, good life for himself in the land of Midian after fleeing for his life from Egypt where he had killed an Egyptian in retaliation for the Egyptian's beating a Hebrew out where the Hebrews were being forced to do hard labor. Moses was now happily married to the daughter of Jethro, the priest of Midian, whose flock Moses was taking care of on this particular pleasant day out in the wilderness. So Moses was perfectly content taking care of Jethro's sheep, and he really had no urgent reason to venture away from the flock just to satisfy his curiosity about a blazing bush.

However, there was something about this burning bush that was mysterious and awe-inspiring and able to arouse Moses' natural curiosity and spiritual sensitivity to the point that Moses simply had to follow the inner urge that had been awakened within him. Because Moses allowed his inner urge to guide his footsteps toward the burning bush, Moses ended up in a special, sacred place where God could speak to him and make known God's plan for Moses to return to Egypt. The encounter and the conversation Moses had with God serve to show us what the dynamics of our own personal contact and conversation with God can be.

First of all, Moses is told to take off his shoes. He is made aware that he is standing on holy ground, a piece of earth that has taken on a sacred dimension. Wherever God meets us, we may become aware that our three dimensional world has taken on a mysterious, additional fourth dimension, a spiritual dimension that can make any three dimensional place become holy ground, sacred and different, whether it be a favorite chair where we sit for our daily prayers and reading of the Bible, or whether it be a bench in a city park or a flower bed in our back yard or a balcony outside a hotel window. Whenever and wherever we feel tuned in and turned on because we and God are now suddenly on the same wave length, any place where this happens becomes supercharged with a fourth dimension, a spiritual dimension that makes an ordinary place suddenly look different to us as a sacred place. For the people of Israel, Mount Horeb, also known as Mount Sinai, was holy ground as a sacred mountain where God could be worshiped, a sacred place where Moses' life took on an additional spiritual dimension as Moses engaged in close level conversation with God and saw the meaning of his life from a new and deeper perspective.

At this sacred mountain, God enables Moses to examine and understand the meaning of his entire life — past, present, and future — from a new point of view. God says to Moses, "I am the God of your father and your forefathers, Abraham, Isaac, and Jacob who followed and served me in the past. I am the God who has a stake in the present day affliction of my people, your kinfolk, held captive in Egypt. And I am the God who wants you to lead my people out of Egypt into a brighter and better future." The God of the past, the present, and the future makes Moses keenly aware of his inescapable connection to his spiritual heritage from the past, his inescapable connection to the terrible present day crisis of the Israelites back in Egypt, and his inescapable connection to a future leadership role enabling God's chosen people to escape from slavery in Egypt. Moses stands on holy ground where the past, present, and future dimensions of his life now take on new meaning provided by the God of the past, the God of the present, and the God of the future.

Regardless of where we pray — in our living room, in our backyard, in our car, in a church sanctuary — any place wherever we happen to meet God becomes for us a sacred place like a holy mountain where we stand on higher ground and holy ground, where our three dimensional lives take on a spiritual fourth dimension, and we, like Moses, are called by God to face up to the true meaning of our past, our present, and our future. Prayer takes us upward to the higher ground and the holy ground of a mountain top experience where from the top of the mountain we are now in a position to look backward in time and see the land of our past far below from which we have been climbing upward since our childhood days. As we look backward in time, we can see from a greater and more mature perspective certain past events and past experiences in our growing up years — the childhood squabbles we had with brothers or sisters or the kids at school, the advice our parents tried to give us which we didn't appreciate at the time. There are those puzzling or perplexing experiences we had years ago which now, from our mountaintop perspective, make much more sense: why during our first job we didn't get the promotion we expected, or why the breakup of a particular friendship was actually a blessing in disguise, or why a decision made by a teacher or a parent or a job supervisor in our behalf now makes sense, even though it seemed really weird at the time. Prayer lifts us up to the higher ground and the holy ground of a perspective whereby puzzling things in our past begin to make more sense and acquire more meaning.

Prayer also lifts us up to the higher ground and the holy ground of a perspective whereby puzzling things in the present day begin to make more sense and acquire more meaning. The spiritual fourth dimension of our mountaintop perspective enables us to look more clearly and more perceptively at a present day situation such as a decision whether or not to get surgery for a bad knee, or whether or not to spend hard earned money to send one of our youngsters with scholastic problems to a private tutor, or whether or not to sell the house and move to a retirement home. And from the top of the sacred mountain we also can look ahead to where the trail down the mountain will take us to a future destination. Although many things are so far off we can't quite get them in clear focus, we still can see tell-tale clues of what our present situation will produce in the future as the result of wise or foolish present day decisions regarding how we invest our savings for a rainy day, or whether or not we follow the doctor's advice regarding our daily diet, or whether or not we have an active or inactive relationship with our local church. When we stand on higher ground and holy ground with a spiritual fourth dimension view of reality, we become much more deeply aware of our lifelong relationship to God — past, present, and future.

But the view of life that comes to us at the holy mountain may be a view that we cannot always accept gladly. God wants Moses to leave the secure, good life of tending sheep and go back to the harsh life in Egypt in order to lead the people of Israel out of captivity. And Moses protests, "Who am I that I should go to Pharoah, and bring the Israelites out of Egypt?" (Exodus 3:11). Like Moses, who was not immediately enthusiastic about his tough assignment to lead the Israelites out of Egypt, we too may receive in our sacred mountain experience an assignment that makes us feel reluctant and inadequate — for example, heading up a church's financial campaign when giving has been at a low ebb, coaching a middle school basketball team whose players have limited athletic ability plus a losing record, or providing home care to an elderly person with Alzheimer's disease and an irritable disposition.

However, like Moses, we too will receive the assurance that God will be with us and that we can trust him to help us. God promised Moses that if he obeyed God and led the Israelites out of Egypt, then Moses would worship once again at this holy mountain. God promises us that we too will have another uplifting sacred mountain experience that will bring us close to God once again, if we do faithfully what God has told us he wants us to do — with God right beside us helping in every way. After we have done our level best in working with the church's financial campaign or the middle school basketball team or an elderly person afflicted with Alzheimer's, we indeed may become thoroughly exasperated by people's ridiculous excuses why they don't give to the church, or we may become extremely discouraged by the slow progress of the basketball team's ability to learn even the simplest basketball basics, or we may feel utterly exhausted whenever an elderly person asks us the very same question over and over and over again. Whenever we have tried to do our level best for God, regardless of how many frustrations we encounter in our God-given assignment, God will see to it that we will worship once again at the holy mountain where once again our weary and worn out, three dimensional existence will be blessed, refreshed, renewed, and uplifted by the grace of God's spiritual fourth dimension.

In response to God's promise that God will be with Moses in Egypt, Moses then asks how he will be able to convince the Israelites that God has really spoken to him. Moses asks God, "What is your name?" In those days the name of a god was regarded as a sign vindicating the god's authority and authenticity. The Hebrew name for God is spelled YHWH, pronounced Yahweh, and it is taken from the Hebrew word *hayah* which means "to be." When we identify God as Yahweh, a name taken from the Hebrew word "to be," we are saying that God is the one authentic God who really is. So when God says, "I AM WHO I AM" (Genesis 3:14),

God is saying to Moses "I really am who I am. I really am who I say I am. I am for real! So go and tell the people of Israel, Moses, that Yahweh, I AM WHO I AM, has sent you to them." Moses knew it would be absolutely essential to show the Israelites that he had the authentic credentials of a true spokesman in behalf of the true God who really is. After all, there are many false prophets who claim they know the true God but whose god actually is the self-centered, trinitarian idol known as "Me, Myself, and I." For example, in the movie *Leap Of Faith*.[1] Steve Martin plays the role of a traveling evangelist who uses electronic trickery to con his audience into taking a leap of faith and donating huge sums of money in hope of being healed. However, when a young man experiences an authentic healing miracle, this authentic event terrifies the phony evangelist, who quickly packs up and leaves town.

Whenever we have an authentic close relationship with the God who is for real, God then is able to transform us into authentic people who are for real. And the best thing that our children or our closest friends can ever say about us is that regardless of all our faults and failures, we are definitely for real. Our children certainly can tell the vital difference between the parents who go with their children to church and the parents who stay home but send their children to church. Only if we are for real will we then, like Moses, become a living proof to our children and anyone else that our God is for real. We are told that Jesus frequently went up into the mountains to pray, whenever he needed the new perspective of a spiritual fourth dimension showing how the past, the present, and the future of his journey through our three dimensional world were measuring up to what God expected of him. Jesus today bids us to walk with him upwards on a mountain trail until we have reached the higher ground and the holy ground where the God who is for real is waiting to give us a renewed life perspective and a refreshed spirit.

---

1. Richard Pearce, director, *Leap Of Faith*, motion picture, Paramount, 1992.

**Proper 18
Pentecost 16
Ordinary Time 23
Exodus 12:1-14**

Saved Through The Blood Of The Lamb

Many times, especially during Lent, we hear that Jesus is the Lamb of God who shed his blood on the cross for our sins. But how do you feel when the doorbell rings, and you open the door, and there is someone holding a Bible who starts up a conversation leading up to questions such as, "Have you been saved? Have you been saved through the blood of the Lamb?" Or how do you feel when you turn on your television and an evangelist pleads with you to accept "the salvation that comes only through the blood of Jesus, the Lamb of God"? Or how would you feel if you were a Hebrew living in ancient Egypt where life was absolutely miserable working out in the hot sun with mortar and bricks, and all the Hebrews were told by Moses to mark the doorposts of their homes with the blood of a lamb in order to escape from the threat of death on the night when the first born child in every Egyptian home would die? It may be very hard for us to believe that anyone's life or anyone's soul can be saved through the blood of a lamb.

An old gospel hymn proclaims that there is "power in the blood of the Lamb."[1] This old hymn maintains that the power of salvation comes to us through the shedding of Christ's blood on the cross. Ask a church member in a church we typically describe as fundamentalist, evangelical, or Pentecostal, and we will probably be told that, yes, there is definitely power in the blood of the Lamb. This churchgoer may have no difficulty whatsoever in believing that through the blood of Jesus shed on the cross God has made the power of his forgiveness and salvation available to us. A churchgoer from a more liberal mainstream denomination may believe that Christ's death and resurrection truly bring us salvation, but this belief may be mixed and mingled with a certain amount of doubt, confusion, and skepticism as to how salvation actually is made available through the cross of Jesus. It is safe to say that many church members from mainstream denominations find no way to make any sense out of the claim that through the blood of Christ shed on the cross God's powerful gift of forgiveness and salvation is made available to us. Just how can there be any power in the blood of the Lamb? Too often churches and pastors have been guilty of simply proclaiming that the cross is God's way of making salvation available, without providing any explanation to make more clear how the death of Christ is able to lead to our salvation.

Before we simply shrug our shoulders and decide that only fundamentalist, evangelical, and Pentecostal Christians can honestly believe that there is power in the blood of the Lamb, we need to try to understand what is being said in the Bible about the ritual of animal sacrifice. Why did the Hebrews in Egypt believe that the blood of a lamb, smeared both on the doorposts and overhead on the lintel, the beam above the doorway, would spare them from the dreadful death which would afflict the Egyptian households? There has to be a much deeper explanation for this than simply that if God saw the blood on the doorway, then God would know for sure that this was a Hebrew household for God to pass over and not an Egyptian household to be afflicted with the death of the firstborn. After all, it is reasonably safe to assume that God already knew which households were Hebrew and which were Egyptian!

A deeper understanding of today's scripture from the book of Exodus takes into consideration why the Hebrews were given such precise, detailed instructions for the first Passover observance. They were told to select an unblemished lamb and mark the doorposts and the lintel with some of the lamb's blood. The sacrifice of a first rate, unblemished lamb instead of a second rate animal was seen as absolutely necessary in order to obtain the Passover blessing of deliverance from death. The Hebrews were told to roast the lamb over the fire, and then prepare and eat the Passover meal in a big hurry, fully clothed with sandals on their feet while holding a staff used when walking. Picture yourself holding a big stick in one hand and trying to eat your food with your other hand! The Hebrews were instructed to eat unleavened bread and to rid their households of all leaven and all food that had been leavened. All this would serve to prepare the Hebrews to face the fact that when they escaped from Egypt they indeed would be in a big hurry. They would have absolutely no time to use leaven to make their bread rise. The painstaking preparation for the Passover observance was intended to deepen and purify the faith of the people not only so that their households would be passed over and spared from death, but also so that the Hebrews would be better prepared for the strong commitment of faith they would need when making the effort to escape from Egypt.

The New Testament understanding of Christ as the Lamb of God is related directly to the Old Testament understanding of how anyone's life or anyone's soul could be saved through the blood of a lamb. If the dynamics of salvation are to become more than just a mumbo-jumbo mystery for us, it is absolutely important to go way back in time and try to understand how the sacrifice of a lamb or the sacrifice of Christ as the Lamb of God made sense to devout believers as a way to make the power of salvation available to God's faithful people. Only then will we be in a position to see how ancient wisdom can be reinterpreted in order to make sense today according to a modern point of view.

First of all, we need to understand that in the Old Testament the blood of a sacrificial animal is regarded as containing the vitality of the life of the animal. The death of a sacrificial lamb is seen, therefore, as an event that releases the vitality of the animal's life as a blessing which brings cleansing and renewal. Frequently in temple worship the priest would take the blood of the sacrificial animal and then sprinkle the altar and also the people with this blood. It was believed and understood that the sacrificial animal's life, vitality, and energy were present in the blood that the priest sprinkles on the altar and the people. This action of sprinkling the blood on the people was seen as making the animal's life, vitality, and energy available to the people as a powerful blessing, a blessing which cleanses the people from their sins and renews the people's spiritual vitality and strength.

This Old Testament viewpoint of the blessing through the sprinkling of the animal's blood is carried over into the first letter of Peter in the New Testament. The Christians to whom this letter is written are described as those "who have been chosen and destined by God the Father and sanctified by the Spirit to be obedient to Jesus Christ *and sprinkled with his blood*" (1 Peter 1:2, italics added). In the New Testament the blood of Christ and the life of Christ are understood as existing together as an inseparable combination. In John 6:53 Jesus says to his listeners, "Unless you eat the flesh of the Son of Man and drink his blood, you have no life in you." Christ's shedding his blood for us is understood as Christ giving the vitality of his life for us. In the service of Holy Communion we drink of the cup which symbolizes the blood of Christ, because the cup symbolizes our receiving the power and the vitality of the life of Christ. The communion cup as a symbol of Christ's blood shed for us is a reminder that through the death of a sacrificial lamb or through the death of Christ as the Lamb of God, spiritual power and spiritual vitality are released and made available to God's faithful people.

Our modern day understanding of the principles of atomic energy and nuclear physics can enable us from a contemporary point of view to appreciate the biblical understanding of how death leads to new life. We are aware that the splitting of an atom leads to a release of power and the start of a nuclear chain reaction. Similarly, the death and resurrection of Christ can be understood as a type of spiritual "nuclear explosion" that released the energy of Christ's life in the form of an ongoing, powerful chain reaction consisting of endless life and endless love. Just as radioactive isotopes of cobalt can be used to treat various types of cancer, so the released energy of the crucified and risen Christ has the healing and cleansing power to cure the cancer of the sinsick soul and give us a new lease on life. Our awareness of the power that comes through the splitting of the atom can lead us to view with grateful appreciation instead of scornful skepticism the biblical understanding of how the death of a sacrificial lamb or the death of Christ as the Lamb of God brings about cleansing and renewal. We need to realize with deepest gratitude that our spiritual ancestors in the Old and New Testament were in touch with something powerfully true when they claimed that through death comes life. Back in the days when the Bible was being written, the language of animal sacrifice was the only language available to God's faithful people to describe the profound mystery of how death in God's hands leads to the miracle of cleansing, the miracle of renewal, the miracle of new life.

What then might be a meaningful Passover experience for us according to our own present day understanding of reality? Perhaps we need to receive instructions from a Jewish rabbi who wrote an article in the weekly religion section of a metropolitan newspaper describing how the Passover observance today is celebrated as a meaningful experience. In his article Rabbi Arthur Nemitoff, the Senior Rabbi at Temple Israel in Columbus, Ohio, explains that at the Passover observance known as the Seder, the flat, unleavened bread with no seasoned flavor is intended to serve as a reminder that life in slavery is flat and tasteless compared to life as the free people God wants his faithful people to be. On the ceremonial Seder plate there are five symbolic foods: 1) a roasted lamb shank bone as a reminder of the lambs slaughtered for food to take on the journey out of Egypt; 2 and 3) an egg and a sprig of parsley as symbols of springtime and the movement out of slavery into freedom; 4) some bitter herbs, usually horseradish, as a reminder of how bitter slavery can be and how much we should fight against it; and 5) a mixture of apples, nuts, honey, wine, and spices called *charoset*, which looks like the mortar used by slave labor to make brick walls in Egypt, but which has a sweet taste showing that freedom and new life are always possible with God's help. Rabbi Nemitoff would teach us that Passover is more than just a time to remember how horrible it was to be slaves in Egypt. Passover is also a time to rededicate ourselves to fighting injustice and persecution in our world today.[2]

The first Passover instituted by Moses in Egypt was intended to prepare the Hebrews to face up to the difficult journey that would take them out of Egypt headed toward the Promised Land. Perhaps in keeping with that first Passover, we also could participate in worship that includes a meal of lamb and unleavened bread which is not eaten leisurely but in a big hurry with one hand on a packed suitcase or some other object used in travel, comparable to the wooden staff a Hebrew was expected to have in hand during the first Passover observance. As we eat our meal and gulp down our food in a big hurry, we can think about the ways in which we are held helplessly captive in our own life situations. We can dedicate ourselves to undertake the difficult journey that will be required to take us out of captivity into the new freedom God wants us to have. To what extent are we held captive in a daily schedule so busy and so overcrowded that again and again we live on a "fast food" diet of microwave meals, ready-mixed, frozen food complete dinners, or whatever we can grab quickly at the nearest McDonald's or Kentucky Fried Chicken? Perhaps our own Passover observance ought to include some typical modern day "fast food" to be eaten in a big hurry as a reminder of our own need to be delivered from a hectic family schedule requiring us to gulp down our food quickly and run out the door to the next big event on our overcrowded schedule with no time for leisurely conversation.

At this Passover meal a cup of grape juice or wine reminds us of the awful journey Jesus took to win freedom for us, carrying his cross through the streets of Jerusalem toward the terrible destination where Christ, the Lamb of God, shed his blood on the cross and died in order that there would be a spiritual "nuclear explosion" to release the power of endless life and endless love in order to make us truly free and no longer captive to sin and death. Yes, we can agree there is powerful truth in the old gospel hymn which insists that "there is power in the blood of the Lamb." We can reinterpret the Bible's ancient understanding of animal sacrifice with the help of today's nuclear age imagery to describe how death leads to life through a powerful chain reaction of endless life and endless love that extends all the way to us from Jesus' death on the cross. Passover, Good Friday, and Easter are a powerful reminder that in God's hands death is forced to trigger an explosive eruption of new life. We in this nuclear age can truly believe there is indeed salvation power in the blood of the Lamb.

1. Lewis E. Jones, "There is Power in the Blood."

2. Rabbi Arthur Nemitoff, "Show-and-taste evokes story behind Passover," *Columbus (Ohio) Dispatch,* March 26, 1999, "Faith and Values" Section D (description of Passover Seder and its significance), p. 2.

**Proper 19
Pentecost 17
Ordinary Time 24
Exodus 14:19-31**

Coming Through In The Clutch

The highest compliment that can be said about an athlete is that he or she can be counted on to come through in the clutch. A baseball player who comes through in the clutch is, for example, the batter who fouls off several bad pitches and then delivers a key base hit to drive in the winning run when there are two outs in the ninth inning. A basketball player who comes through in the clutch is, for example, the player who comes through to score the winning basket with only seconds left on the clock after the coach has set up a play to make sure the ball is fed to this player that everyone is counting upon. We count on key people to come through in the clutch in many other areas besides athletics. The story has been told about a passenger in a small airplane whose pilot had collapsed from a heart attack and who needed very calm and simple instructions over the radio from an airport flight controller how to bring that airplane down safely. That passenger and that flight controller were in a clutch situation where everything had to fall into place perfectly if, step by step, finally, that airplane could be able to make a safe landing.

Today's Old Testament Lesson could be described as a story telling how God enabled Moses to come through in the clutch, so that the Israelites were able to escape through the sea's divided waters with the Egyptian chariots in hot pursuit. In sports the pressure is on a key player to come through in the clutch when the hometown fans have been mean and nasty toward this superstar, hissing and booing and jeering, because they think this star athlete has been failing to come through as expected. Moses had been taking all kinds of heat from the Israelites who had started out with him to escape from Egypt but who now could see the Egyptian chariots rapidly coming up from behind. Like angry fans in the bleachers booing and yelling insults, the Israelites cried out to Moses, "What have you done to us, bringing us out of Egypt? ... (It) would have been better for us to serve the Egyptians than to die in the wilderness" (Exodus 14:11b, 12b). But Moses didn't lose his cool, because God had already told him that it was God's plan to let the Egyptians chase the Israelites, so that God could show the Egyptians that Yahweh and not the Egyptian gods was the true God.

We all know how this story turned out. Moses stretched out his hand over the sea as God commanded him to do. Then God sent a strong east wind to divide the waters so that the Israelites walked on dry land to safety. Then when the Egyptian chariots followed the Israelites, Moses stretched out his hand once again. God made the wind cease so that the waters returned, and the Egyptians were drowned in the sea. It has been suggested in *Ripley's Believe It Or Not* and other sources that this so-called miracle can be explained scientifically as a natural event that definitely could happen, given the proper combination of wind and tide. Even so, Old Testament scholars tell us the real miracle God performed is the perfect timing of this amazing event, so that the waters were divided right at the critical moment when the Israelites had to escape from the approaching chariots. The additional miracle is the perfect timing so that the waters returned after the Egyptians and their chariots had gone so far in chasing the Israelites that they could not pull back before being engulfed by the returning waters. God's miraculous action produced the perfect timing for the parting of the sea and also the perfect timing for the return of the waters.

The story of Moses leading his people through the sea to safety is the story of a situation where God's chosen people were rescued only when Moses follows some very strange instructions to stretch out his hand over the sea. The Bible has many episodes in which the instructions for getting out of a predicament or resolving a problem are indeed very strange. Joshua is instructed to take his army marching one complete circuit around the city of Jericho for six days in a row. Then on the seventh day Joshua and his army must march around the city seven times when, with a mighty shout from the Israelites, the high wall of the city would now come tumbling down. Naaman the leper finds it extremely strange when Elisha, the prophet, tells him to wash himself in the Jordan River seven times. Naaman does so and his leprosy goes away. The disciples of Jesus must have found it very strange when prior to his ride into Jerusalem on Palm Sunday, Jesus tells his disciples to go into a village where he promises they will find a young colt for Jesus to ride on, a colt that has never been ridden before, and then, without asking anyone's permission, the disciples are to untie the colt and bring it back to Jesus.

Sometimes in our own lives we are asked to follow strange instructions or take part in risky maneuvers in a high risk situation when success is not at all possible unless all the details fall into place. In baseball the suicide squeeze play and the safety squeeze play are high risk strategies that are apt to be used only if a team desperately needs to score a run to tie or win a game. The suicide squeeze play is a very risky maneuver that requires a baserunner at third base to start running as hard as possible toward home plate before the batter has had a chance to make contact with the ball thrown by the pitcher. When the pitcher throws the ball, the suicide squeeze play requires the batter to try to bunt the ball instead of swinging away at the pitch. If the batter fails to hit the ball, then the catcher has the ball and can easily tag out the runner coming home from third base.[1] That's the suicide squeeze. The safety squeeze play is less risky because it requires the batter to make contact and bunt the ball successfully before the runner at third base starts running toward home. Much more risky is the suicide squeeze when the runner takes off for home from third base without first knowing whether or not the batter can make contact with the ball thrown by the pitcher.

In various high risk life situations requiring high risk strategies and procedures, we may have to attempt a "suicide squeeze play" instead of a "safety squeeze play" without any reduction whatsoever in the risk that we might fail in our effort. In medicine the risks of major surgery may require that the surgeon take drastic steps and follow very carefully the precise steps for an extremely high risk procedure when there is no foolproof guarantee that this risky procedure will be successful for a patient who has everything to lose if no surgery is attempted. The decision to help a new church get started and organized in a community may require a denomination to go way out on a limb and put up a financial loan before there is any guarantee that the church's minister will be able to enlist enough new members to build a vibrant and vital congregation. Parents know the nervous stomach of providing last minute instructions and then handing over the keys of the family car to a teenager who at some point needs to attain the experience of driving alone without being accompanied either by an anxious mother or a hypercritical father.

For the Israelites pursued by the Egyptian chariots, trapped between "the devil and the deep blue sea," the maneuver to get the Israelites to safety could be described as a "suicide squeeze play." Like the baserunner taking off for home plate before the batter has a chance to make contact with the ball, Moses stretched his hand out over the sea, trusting that God would then follow through by making the waters divide. This maneuver was in no way a safety squeeze play in which God made the waters begin to divide before Moses stretched out his hand in plain sight of all those skeptical, frightened, angry Israelites. No, here was a suicide squeeze play with Moses keeping his cool under heavy pressure to come through in the clutch, trusting that God would not let him fail before all the Israelites who were watching closely with critical eyes, who had given Moses plenty of angry, heated flak, and who were dead sure that Moses had gotten them into a tight squeeze from which no escape was possible.

There may be many questions and doubts stirred up by the story of how God commanded the wind and the sea to aid the escape of the Israelites from Egypt. After all, if God was able to come through in the clutch and make the forces of nature serve his purpose in behalf of God's chosen people, then what exactly is God doing when hurricanes, floods, earthquakes, and tidal waves bring death to innocent people? There are many unanswered questions asking why evil can exist in a world created by a God we say is good. In Romans chapter 8, Paul mentions the natural disaster of famine, people starving to death due to a natural disaster such as no rainfall producing a severe drought, destroying all the crops people count upon for food to stay alive. And in Romans chapter 8, Paul very boldly raises the question and answers the question of "where is God when bad things happen to good people." The Apostle Paul would speak to us today in words very similar to his words in Romans chapter 8: "Will hardship, or distress, or persecution, or nakedness, or peril, or sword, or even an overwhelming disaster at the hands of the forces of nature such as a famine or hurricanes, floods, earthquakes, or tidal waves ever succeed in separating us from the love of God? No, even in all these terrible, terrible things we are more than conquerors through him who loved us" (Romans 8:35, 37).

In other words, Paul would tell us that God always makes something good come out of even the very worst situations in which bad things happen to good people, when something truly heartbreaking happens which God in no way wants to happen to anyone. For instance, a child is born with serious medical problems that cannot be eliminated, an elderly person's caretaker steals all the hard-earned life savings, a hurricane or a tidal wave wipes out entire villages of people who have lived on next to nothing. In many truly heartbreaking, terrible situations such as these, God often uses the church and church members like you and me as God's way to make goodness triumph over evil. God may ask the church to come up with volunteers to assist the parents of a physically or mentally challenged child. God may ask the church to help find an attorney to assist the elderly person who has been victimized by a caretaker. God many times calls upon Church World Service and our denomination's mission outposts throughout the world to step in whenever a natural disaster has been truly devastating.

In one way or another God does come through in the clutch even when our life situation has turned into a suicide squeeze play, a situation in which we are compelled to go first and make a leap of faith, trusting that God then will follow through with his promise to hold out his steady hands to catch us, and keep us from falling, and keep us from failing. The story of Moses leading the Israelites through the sea to safety has become the scriptural basis of a verse from a well-known hymn: "When through the deep waters I call thee to go, the rivers of woe shall not thee overflow; For I will be near thee, thy troubles to bless, and sanctify to thee thy deepest distress."[2] No matter what kind of tight squeeze would leave us helplessly trapped, God promises to lead us safely through even the deepest waters to some kind of victorious outcome. In one way or another our most terrible experiences of crucifixion are always followed by some form of triumphant resurrection, as God again and again and again comes through in the clutch.

---

1. The illustration regarding the "suicide squeeze play" and the "safety squeeze play" has been written in an effort to make it understandable (I hope!) to any persons who may be completely unfamiliar with baseball. Perhaps it may be helpful if the preacher uses hand motions to illustrate bunting the ball, swinging away at the pitch, and tagging out the runner.

2. "How Firm A Foundation," "K" in John Rippon's *A Selection Of Hymns*, 1787, alt.; FOUNDATION, Early American melody, harmonized by Charles H. Heaton, 1928.

**Proper 20
Pentecost 18
Ordinary Time 25
Exodus 16:2-15**

Living On One Day's Rations

Preparing for an outdoor adventure of hiking, camping, mountain climbing, or canoeing includes planning how the food supply is to be managed. This will require deciding how much food is needed in order to last the entire trip. It's critically important to know how much food can be carried in a back pack or stashed in a canoe. Of course the food supply for a camping venture may be much less difficult to plan, if there just happens to be a grocery store within easy traveling distance of the campsite! However, careful planning for a hiking expedition over the many miles of the Appalachian Trail may require figuring how packages of food can be shipped to certain pickup points along the route. Can you imagine an experienced hiker, camper, mountain climber, or canoe paddler being satisfied with whatever food supply arrangements had been set up for the Israelites out in the wilderness headed on their way from Egypt back toward their home country? Nearly two months had passed since the Israelites had left Egypt, they had completely run out of food, and they had absolutely no idea where the next meal was coming from. The Israelites complained bitterly to Moses and Aaron, "If only we had died by the hand of God in the land of Egypt, when we sat by the kettles full of meat and ate our fill of bread; for you have brought us out into this wilderness to kill this whole assembly with hunger" (Exodus 16:3). But God's response to the moaning and groaning of the Israelites was not to have an angel or a helicopter fly in with a big supply of food guaranteed to last several days until the next scheduled drop-off.

No, God's response was simply to provide one day's rations one day at a time!

God told Moses that each day there would be just enough food provided to last for one day, while on the sixth day there would be enough food for two days. The arrangement for the sixth day made it possible for the people to have enough food to make it through the holy sabbath when there would be no gathering of food allowed. The daily ration would include a fresh supply of meat in the evening and a fresh supply of manna or "bread from heaven" in the morning. The meat consisted of small birds, quails that flew into the Israelites' camp. These quails were on their regular migratory route northward, and migration for these little birds was an exhausting trip done in separate stages giving the quails a chance to stop and rest. When these small birds stopped at the Israelites' camp, they were so exhausted that it was very easy to catch them and gather them off the ground.[1]

The manna or the "bread from heaven" has been described and explained two different ways. A longstanding traditional explanation has been that the manna was a sticky substance produced by the tamarisk bush. However, a scientific study has led to the conclusion that what was called manna is actually a liquid honeydew substance released by two types of insects which thrive on the sap they extract from certain plants. This sap is rich in carbohydrates but low in nitrogen content, and so the insects must consume a large amount of sap in order to get enough nitrogen needed to maintain the insects' body metabolism. The extra sap is released by the insects as a liquid honeydew substance which quickly changes in the dry desert air into drops of sticky solids that accumulate on the ground with a gritty, chrystallized texture. This "bread from heaven" has been collected from the ground since ancient times and referred to as "manna." The Israelites learned very quickly that manna could not be stored indefinitely, because it would spoil very quickly and attract worms. This is one reason why, according to Old Testament tradition, the Israelites had to be content with living on one day's rations one day at a time, with the one exception that God provided an extra supply of manna to last through the sabbath day.[2]

The familiar request in the prayer of our Savior, "Give us this day our daily bread" (Matthew 6:11), probably has some historic roots in Israel's understanding that one day's supply of bread and meat, available only one day at a time, was completely sufficient to guarantee the Israelites' survival in the wilderness.[3] God wanted to give the Israelites only one day's supply of food each day as a way to test their willingness to become totally dependent upon God and to put their complete trust in God's faithfulness. God said to Moses, "In that way I will test them, whether they will follow my instruction or not" (Exodus 16:4b). So when we pray in the prayer of our Savior, "Give us this day our daily bread," we are indicating our complete trust in God's faithfulness to take care of our bread and butter survival needs just one day at a time.

But the idea of one day's rations one day at a time may not go over very well today. It has been said that our prosperous society is afflicted with a "social disease" known as "Affluenza,"[4] the insatiable, greedy, self-centered desire to make our affluent way of life one big shopping spree for every luxury and convenience possible — digital cameras no longer requiring film to take pictures, the computer's Internet advantages of online banking, stock market trades, or online catalog purchases. It's not enough for a car simply to drive you where you want to go. Now automobiles can be loaded with all kinds of electronic controls for giving travel directions for the route you wish to follow or setting each passenger's individual air temperature comfort level. The wish list for greater luxury and greater convenience goes on and on and on. Some economics experts have said that there are simply not enough available resources in the world that can be redistributed so that the residents of the poverty-stricken areas of the world could ever be elevated to our own superabundant standard of living. Now this may be a hard piece of bread for us to chew on or swallow, but the prayer "Give us this day our daily bread" could come to mean this: "O God, let the world's prosperous people become willing to lower their standard of living and become content to live on just what is absolutely necessary to thrive and survive each day, so that extra resources can then be reallocated to the world's poverty-stricken people whose daily rations are far less than even the bare minimum of what is required for anyone to thrive and survive." After all, the prayer "Give us this day our daily bread" refers not just to you and me. "Give *us* this day" refers to all God's children as "us," including especially those children of God who have to scrounge each day through garbage dumps to find the huge heaps of food wasted and thrown away by restaurants, cruise ships, school cafeterias, and all the rest of us.

We might wonder just how satisfied the Israelites were with the daily rations provided by God. When the Israelites saw the manna on the ground, they were puzzled and wondered what it was. The Israelites asked the question "What is it?" which, translated into Hebrew, is to ask the question *Man hu*? According to ancient tradition, this question *Man hu*? explains how the Hebrew name "manna" was given to the "bread from heaven" that appeared on the ground each day, so strange and so unfamiliar in its appearance the Israelites asked themselves, "*Man hu*? What is it?" And so the word "manna" eventually became a well-known metaphor in the Bible and in Christian tradition referring to the blessings of God's grace and providence as "manna" or "bread from heaven."[5]

We know that the Israelites had been a group of unhappy campers out in the wilderness, and unhappy campers often are picky eaters not easily satisfied with what is served on the dinner table. Anyone who has ever been in charge of a group of kids at summer camp knows that the favorite indoor sport in the dining hall is complaining about the food in one way or another. When the Israelites saw the unfamiliar manna, really weird-looking stuff, lying on the ground, the Israelites asked, "What is it?" Likewise, when young campers in the dining hall take just one look at something unfamiliar the cook has served up which in no way resembles anything in Mom's kitchen back home, immediately there is the disgusted look and the horrified question, "What is *that*?" Any cool drink made from Kool-Aid or some other powdered drink source has often been given the name "bug juice" by a young camper crowd of dining hall gourmet critics. So perhaps the Israelites' children as typical picky eaters said to each other, "What is *that*?" when they saw this really weird-looking bread from heaven. And who knows what kind of colorful, yukky name for this food these finicky kids may have come up with, especially if this manna came from "bug juice" actually produced by bugs! Although a lot of freeze-dried or dehydrated food prepared for camping expeditions is really very tasty and very flavorful, many adults, nevertheless, have unpleasant memories of various kinds of field rations served in outdoor situations. Many a veteran of the armed services has said after discharge and return home, "Don't ever serve up any of that miserable tasting stuff! I had my fill of that in the military!" Grown-ups, as well as children, have been heard to complain if the "same old thing" is served up again and again at the dinner table! So we might well wonder whether the Israelites out in the wilderness continued to be a bunch of unhappy campers, especially if every meal day after day after day featured the same old thing — roasted bird and sticky bread.

Moses and Aaron made it very clear to the Israelites that all their moaning and groaning was not really directed against Moses and Aaron. No, the Israelites needed to realize that it was God who was the target of the people's complaints. During the Israelites' journey through the wilderness, the presence of God was made known to the Israelites in the form of a pillar of cloud by day and a pillar of fire by night. Very soon after the Israelites have made their loud complaints to Moses and Aaron, the radiant glory of God then appears like sunlight breaking through a cloud as a fiery, glowing indicator that God is definitely near at hand. After the Israelites have seen this powerful evidence of God's presence, God speaks to Moses and says, "I have heard the complaining of the Israelites; say to them, 'At twilight you shall eat meat, and in the morning you shall have your fill of bread; then you shall know that I am your God, the God who is truly in charge of your life' " (Exodus 16:12).

Moses and Aaron had tried again and again to get the Israelites to realize that their unhappy camper complaints reflected a lack of trust in God's ability to provide what truly was needed in order to thrive and survive. One of the symptoms of the societal disease of "Affluenza" may be the symptom of complaining like unhappy campers whenever our affluent existence has its kinks and its quirks. We live in an affluent age when our technology is expected to speed things up for our convenience. But we all fuss and fume about that slow-as-molasses traffic light that always gets stuck on red forever during our usual travel route from home to the office. The telephone becomes especially irritating when a recorded message says, "If you want a statement of your account, press one. If you want to order a new product, press two," and finally, after several more options, if you really want to speak to a live body instead of a frustrating machine, "press zero." It really doesn't take very much in an affluent society for even the petty inconveniences and the minor irritations of an imperfect world to become absolutely intolerable. Whenever our justifiable and yet trivial complaints about the flaws of our technology begin to get the best of us, we very easily become unhappy campers who have lost touch with the God who watches over us at all times to make sure that our real survival needs are being met.

There are times God has absolutely nothing new to say to us in answer to our prayers. Instead God often says, "My grace is sufficient for all your daily needs." The verse of a familiar hymn says very clearly what God may want to say to us if we really are so aware of our biggest bellyaches that we have completely forgotten our biggest blessings: "How firm a foundation, ye saints of the Lord, is laid for your faith in his excellent word! What more can he say than to you he hath said, to you who for refuge to Jesus have fled?"[6] What more could God say to the Israelites who were grumbling and groaning like unhappy campers about their miserable lot out in the wilderness? What more can God say to us whenever our irritable complaining is a tell-tale symptom of that addictive ailment known as "Affluenza"? God patiently but firmly says to us over and over and over again, "You can learn to thrive and survive on your daily bread from heaven one day at a time."

---

1. Cf., W. S. McCollough, "Quail" article in *The Interpreter's Dictionary Of The Bible: K-Q* (New York: Abingdon Press, 1962), p. 973.

2. Cf., J. L. Mihelic, "Manna" article in *The Interpreter's Dictionary Of The Bible: K-Q* (New York: Abingdon Press, 1962), pp. 259-260.

3. Cf., J. Edgar Park, "Exposition" for Exodus in *The Interpreter's Bible Volume 1* (New York: Abingdon Press, 1952), pp. 952-953.

4. Cf., *Affluenza*, television show, PBS, 1997.

5. Cf., J. Coert Rylaarsdam, "Exegesis" for Exodus in *The Interpreter's Bible Volume 1* (New York: Abingdon Press, 1952), p. 953.

6. "How Firm A Foundation," "K" in John Rippon's *A Selection Of Hymns*, 1787, alt.; FOUNDATION, Early American Melody, harmonized by Charles H. Heaton, 1928.

**Proper 21
Pentecost 19
Ordinary Time 26
Exodus 17:1-7**

Does God Help Those Who Help Themselves?

People can survive longer without food than they can survive without water. The book of Exodus tells us that the Israelites had arrived at a place out in the wilderness where they had no water supply whatsoever, and they were getting so desperate that they were ready to really tear into Moses. "Give us water to drink," they demanded of Moses (Exodus 17:2a). Even though God had been faithfully providing the traveling Israelites their daily food supply of manna and meat, the Israelites were quick to lose patience and they argued with Moses, "Why did you bring us out of Egypt, to kill us and our children and our livestock with thirst?" (Exodus 17:3). It often doesn't take very much at all for a group to lose confidence in their leader, even if the leader has had an excellent track record for a long period of time. Just ask any football coach whose team loses a critical game after an outstanding win-loss record. All too often the fans and the alumni are no longer captivated by the glory of yesterday's great achievements. Their fickle attitude is expressed in the well-known cynical complaint, "So what have you done for me today?" Even if the coach receives a vote of confidence from the athletic director or the college president, this still will not satisfy many disgruntled fans and alumni. And even though day after day Moses' leadership had been given a vote of confidence by none other than God, there was no way Moses could put a stop to the Israelites' complaints by asking them, " 'Why do you quarrel with me? Why do you test (our God)?' (Exodus 17:2b). Why have you lost faith in the God whose faithfulness to you has been demonstrated time and time again day after day?" Because of the grumbling and the groaning of the Israelites over the lack of water, the wilderness location where this took place received a name — Massah and Meribah — a name taken from the Hebrew words for "testing" and "quarreling."

We know how this story turns out: God turned on the water, and nobody died of thirst! But the essential meaning of the story for us depends upon whether we are reading the original version of the story in the book of Exodus or a later version of the same story in the book of Numbers. The main theme of the Exodus story is to point out the Israelites' lack of faith in God's care for them. They complain bitterly that there is no water, while Moses remains faithful to God and defends God's faithfulness. Moses, as God's steadfast, faithful servant, produces water after striking the rock with his rod as ordered by God. However, in Numbers a different Old Testament writer who is familiar with the earlier Exodus story has turned things completely around to show — surprise! surprise! — Moses lacking in faith disobeying God! Unlike the writer of the Exodus story, the writer of the Numbers story regards the Israelites' complaint about the water shortage as a perfectly legitimate gripe delivered in a reasonable way. In this writer's opinion, Moses makes the mistake of regarding the people's complaint as one more typical outrageous sinful act of rebellion against God. In the Numbers version of the story God does not tell Moses to strike the rock with his rod. Instead, God instructs Moses simply to give a verbal command telling the rock to produce water.

But instead of obeying God's instructions to give a verbal command to the rock, Moses loses his patience with both the people and with God. Moses explodes with anger, "Listen, you rebels, shall we bring water for you out of this rock?" (Numbers 20:10b). Then, like a frustrated car owner kicking the tires when things aren't going right out on the road, Moses angrily vents his frustration by striking the rock with his rod. Although God is greatly displeased with Moses, the rock produces water because God simply did not want the people to die of thirst out in the hot climate of the wilderness. But striking the rock with the rod shows a lack of trust in God because Moses does not have either the commitment or the patience to follow God's precise instructions simply to give a verbal command to the rock. The consequence of Moses' action for disobeying God's instructions is that God tells him he will never be allowed to cross over into the Promised Land. In the Numbers version of the Massah and Meribah story, God says to Moses and his brother Aaron, "Because you did not trust in me, to show my holiness before the eyes of the Israelites, therefore you shall not bring this assembly into the land that I have given them" (Numbers 20:12).

It has been suggested that the main purpose of the Numbers story is to select and describe a specific event in the history of Israel that could serve as the reason and the explanation why Moses was not allowed to cross over into the Promised Land before he died. The Numbers story says that Moses' failure to reach the Promised Land was because of his act of sinful disobedience at the waters of Massah and Meribah. We really have no way to decide whether Exodus or Numbers is more accurate in describing what actually happened at Massah and Meribah. Regardless of whether Exodus or Numbers has the more accurate version of what actually happened when Moses produced water from the rock, the story in Exodus points out something true that did happen again and again and again in the history of the Israelites' many years of wandering through the wilderness toward the Promised Land. The Exodus story describes the Israelites as not trusting God in spite of all the many amazing and marvelous things God had done to bring them safely through the sea and provide daily rations of meat and manna to eat. Psalm 95 indicates that God became so displeased with the Israelites in the wilderness that God would not allow the current generation of Israelites who were the original group that had fled from Egypt to reach the Promised Land. Only a later generation of Israelites would cross over into the Promised Land. In Psalm 95 the Psalmist issues a call to worship and obedience and says, "O that today you would listen to (God's) voice! Do not harden your hearts, as at Meribah, as on the day at Massah in the wilderness, when your ancestors tested me and put me to the proof, though they had seen my work. For forty years I loathed that generation and said 'They are a people whose hearts go astray, and they do not regard my ways.' Therefore in my anger I swore, 'they shall not enter my rest' " (Psalm 95:7b-11).

We know how frustrating it is at home when no water comes out after we turn on the faucet and the water supply is down to nothing for any number of reasons — a frozen or broken water line, a plugged or corroded water pipe, a broken or burned-out pump in a well. Even if the situation is something we know from experience definitely will be fixed as soon as possible, sometimes we end up griping and groaning non-stop in an irritated manner to our family or the plumber or the city water department or the pump repair service and even God. And God is not necessarily displeased when we complain to God in an exasperated, irritated manner. The Psalms provide several examples of complaints directed toward God. Psalm 142 says, "With my voice I cry to [God]; with my voice I make supplication to [God]. I pour out my complaint ... I tell my trouble before [God]" (Psalm 142:1-2). But Psalm 142 then assumes that God can be trusted to respond to the complaint and the Psalmist says to God, "You are my refuge, my portion in the land of the living ... [You] will deal bountifully with me" (Psalm 142:5, 7). The writer of the Exodus version of the Massah and Meribah story would maintain that the Israelites went way, way too far in their complaints, because they angrily accused Moses directly and God indirectly of allowing them to stumble and tumble into their terrible predicament. Their intense anger is so out of control that Moses fears for his life, and he complains to God, "What shall I do with this people? They are almost ready to stone me" (Exodus 17:4).

Like the Israelites in the Exodus story, we too can be tempted to accuse God of falling asleep on the job, even when God repeatedly has demonstrated his faithfulness. For example, regardless of how often God has made sure that our paycheck has enabled us to make it through the end of the month, the tremendous pressure of a tight financial squeeze can cause us to hit the panic button with uncontrollable outrage as if God has let us down whenever the usual payday shows up and then for some reason no check arrives in the mail or the payroll department's computer has crashed unexpectedly. We also can be tempted to lose patience and take matters into our own hands such as what Moses in the Numbers version of the Massah and Meribah story did when he struck the rock angrily with his rod instead of simply giving a verbal command as God had told him to do. And it can be very easy for us to justify our impulsive actions by telling ourselves, "God helps those who help themselves." According to this traditional saying, we really don't need to wait for God to guide us and help us. Instead we can take matters into our own hands, and we can go out and make something positive happen, trusting that God will bless whatever we do, because "God helps those who help themselves."

In our churches we are guided much more often than we might realize by the attitude that "God helps those who help themselves." Like Moses in the book of Numbers version of the Massah and Meribah story, churches sometimes lose patience and try to make things happen instead of giving God the first chance to guide our decisions and actions. For example, let us suppose that our church is concerned about the needs of low income families or senior citizens or teenagers. As a church we might become very eager to decide what service projects we could do that definitely will make a visible, positive difference, especially if the hour is running late in the evening and our planning group is getting tired and weary and extremely anxious to wrap things up and head home. So we quickly adopt a project such as collecting clothing for low income families or volunteering for the senior citizen "meals on wheels" program or raising money to send teenagers to church camp without first asking in prayer for God to show us what exactly are the real needs of low income families, senior citizens, or teenagers that God would assign specifically to us. We may assume that God certainly will approve and endorse the projects we have chosen, because, after all, "God helps those who help themselves."

At this point you may be thinking, "Hey, pastor, what's wrong with a church gathering clothes for the needy or taking meals to shut-ins or sending kids to church camp? In this terribly complicated world, pastor, at least there are some simple, positive, obvious things we can do that certainly God would approve." It can be said that, yes, God does bless and empower projects such as gathering clothing for the needy or transporting "meals on wheels" to the elderly or raising summer camp scholarship money for teenagers. But God is definitely displeased whenever a church quickly and repeatedly jumps into simple projects of positive action as an easy way out which avoids examining thoroughly and carefully the most stubborn, critical, and complex problems in the life of a community. Instead of limiting our service projects to gathering clothing for the needy or transporting "meals on wheels" to elderly shut-ins or raising summer camp scholarship money, the churches in a community may be asked by God to examine and tackle, first and foremost, some much more difficult issues such as the overcrowded open shelters for the homeless or the inadequate quality of life for many nursing home residents or the crisis of teenagers taking guns and knives to school. Now these are indeed very difficult "hard rock" issues that can seem just too overwhelming for us to face. Indeed life is filled with difficult "hard rock" issues that can leave us feeling helplessly "trapped between a rock and a hard place."

The Massah and Meribah stories in Exodus and Numbers are both worth reading. They serve to point out the "double jeopardy" of two temptations to which we are extremely vulnerable whenever we feel that in our lives the well has run dry and we have ended up "trapped between a rock and a hard place." Once we fall victim to the first temptation to accuse God of falling asleep on the job, we then become very susceptible to the second temptation which is to tell ourselves that "God helps those who help themselves" as we quickly take matters into our own hands rather than patiently place our survival needs in God's hands. God can make even the most stubborn rocks of life's most complicated situations produce sooner or later the miracle of fresh water. We need to discover what God can do and what God will do to make rocks produce water, whenever we humbly confess that the well has run dry and we are trapped helplessly between a rock and a hard place, truly unable to help ourselves and truly dependent upon God's mercy.

**Proper 22
Pentecost 20
Ordinary Time 27
Exodus 20:1-4, 7-9, 12-20**

When God Is Not "User Friendly"

Someone has suggested that if we simply posted the Ten Commandments on the wall in every school building, it would surely help to improve the moral climate in our schools and counteract the terrible and tragic tendencies of youth to resort to drugs, guns, and violent behavior. It has been said that if we would all simply follow the Ten Commandments, the world would be a much better place in which to live! But the Ten Commandments are not simple to follow. The Ten Commandments are not a collection of "user friendly" rules and regulations that are simple to understand and easy to put into practice. In fact, the Ten Commandments provide ample evidence that in many ways God is not a user friendly God who makes it as easy as possible for us to do whatever God wants us to do.[1]

Take, for example, the first and second of the Ten Commandments. God says, "I am the Lord your God, who brought you out of the house of Egypt, out of the house of slavery; you shall have no other gods before me" (Exodus 20:2-3). This is a God who abruptly says in the strongest, loudest language possible, "Listen here, O Israel! I am your God who rescued you from slavery in Egypt. And I am not asking you, I am not pleading with you; I am telling you and commanding you — you shall have no other gods before me. This means that you shall not make for yourself a cheap idol to worship as an easy way out from my demands and my commandments. No ifs, ands, or buts!" This language is really strong stuff! This God could care less whether or not the people of

Israel find their relationship with God to be comfortable, cozy, and user friendly.

And it makes sense for God to spell out the laws of the Ten Commandments like a stern father or mother laying down the law to children who need a dose of firm discipline. The people of Israel out in the wilderness had behaved too often like whining, bellyaching, unhappy campers. Instead of trusting God to take care of them, they had complained and complained to Moses that they would have been much better off back in Egypt than to be stranded out in the wilderness with no obvious supply of food or water. When we realize the people of Israel repeatedly behaved childishly out in the wilderness, we can understand why God set forth the Ten Commandments and laid down the law using the strongest language possible: "I am the God who brought you out of slavery in Egypt, and don't you dare turn to other gods or try to escape my demands by creating and worshiping a handcarved pagan idol which is less than God."

In many ways we may want our God to be a God who is 100 percent user friendly with no awesome dimensions of mystery, holiness, and power that cause us to feel uncomfortable or experience growing pains. Now it is good when certain things are user friendly — for example, a set of written instructions inside the box that tells us in plain and simple language how to assemble the various parts, pieces, and sections of the product — a set of bookshelves, a child's tricycle or scooter, or a plastic gadget known as a hose reel for storing rubber hose we use to water our flowers or wash the car. And we have good reason to get upset when certain things are not user friendly — for example, the fine print details of a contract for buying a new car or an insurance policy, or the complicated instructions that the IRS often expects one to follow in doing one's taxes. But to want our God to be completely user friendly is to want a God who is less than God, a God whose instructions and commandments never challenge us to change our ways or grow in maturity and character.

All too easily the God we worship in church can be only one of the many gods we worship. If we put so much into our job that we have very little quality time left to spend with our children, then we are making financial security the god that controls us and dictates to us. If our charge card accounts are typically greater than what we can pay off completely in a month's time, then perhaps the god that controls us and dictates to us is our enormous appetite for all the expensive goodies and gadgets the American economy can offer us. What does it say about us if we frequently look anxiously in the mirror to be on the watch for new wrinkles as signs of aging, or if we volunteer year after year to be the head honcho of a fund-raising drive that drains our energy but surely looks good on our resume and always gets our name in the newspapers, or if we continue to stash away in our overstuffed closets the very latest fashion styles that the "in crowd" says are an absolute must? All this says that perhaps the god that controls us and dictates to us is a "golden boy" or "golden girl" self-image very similar to the pagan golden calf that the Israelites worshiped instead of the one true God. But the one true God insists, in the strongest language possible, that we throw all our golden idols and all our cheap user friendly gods out in the trash heap where all useless junk belongs.

The third commandment continues to make it clear that we are to give full respect to God and take seriously just who our God is. The third commandment has something more in mind than simply a prohibition against cursing and profanity when it says, "You shall not make wrongful use of the name of the Lord your God" (Exodus 20:7). The people of Israel came to understand that to speak of God by name, to utter the holy name "Yahweh," was to call upon God to be fully present and powerful in the midst of the life of the people. Wrongful use of God's name means using God's name in a way that shows lack of reverent respect and lack of full regard for the God who is holy and supreme by calling upon God to do something that is not in character with God's purpose. For example, the familiar, obscene, angry cusswords that literally call upon God to condemn something or someone are words literally asking God to give powerful support to our petty, spiteful desire to vent our anger and our frustration toward something or someone. The third commandment makes clear that God is not a convenient, handy means for accomplishing whatever goal or purpose we have in mind.

The wrongful use of God's name can actually start very innocently at an early age. When a child prayed, "O God, make Philadelphia the capital of the United States," the listening parent asked, "Why did you pray that?" The child replied, "Because that's the answer I put down on my history test." Now certainly what the child said may not seem absolutely horrible, but from the earliest age on up we need to be taught what are the right ways and the wrong ways to call upon God by name. We indeed use the name of God wrongfully if we ask God to help our favorite football team defeat the team from another school, a team whose fans also may be asking God to help their team defeat our team. And it certainly would serve everyone right, if the game were to end in a tie, regardless of any overtime period designed to be a tie-breaker! The third commandment makes it clear that it is absolutely wrong to call upon God by name either in a way that is grossly profane or in a way that is crudely trivial and cheap.

The familiar saying, "Let go and let God," comes to mind as we reflect upon the meaning of the fourth commandment to "remember the sabbath day and keep it holy" (Exodus 20:8). We are to let go of our workaholic tendencies to keep busy, busy, busy. We are to make time to worship God and let God have our undivided attention, and we are to let God have time to recharge our drained sources of energy. Contrary to what the scribes and Pharisees in Jesus' time tended to think about the sabbath, the main purpose of the sabbath was not to maintain a strict system of sabbath "blue laws" and prohibitions regarding what was acceptable or not acceptable to do on the sabbath. Even though it made the scribes and Pharisees absolutely furious, Jesus healed a man's withered hand on the sabbath and asked his enemies, "Is it lawful to do good or to do harm on the sabbath, to save life or to destroy it?" (Luke 6:9). And so in accord with how Jesus made the sabbath a time for healing, the sabbath is time set aside for a deep level healing of the hurts we have picked up in life's jungle warfare. Our spiritual batteries get a deep level recharge on the sabbath so that we are made ready to travel onward in the next stretch of whatever wilderness journey is in store for us in the week ahead. Churches today are offering Saturday night worship and other opportunities for spiritual renewal besides the traditional Sunday morning hour, especially when there is no simple user friendly sabbath solution for those who must undertake weekend work assignments in law enforcement or at hospitals, ski resorts, or real estate agencies. The sabbath commandment may be regarded rightly as not at all user friendly when, regardless of how demanding your workload is, you are being told you must do somehow what truly may be very hard to do, and that is — you must take time somehow for physical rest and spiritual renewal. Certainly the sabbath commandment offers absolutely no flimsy user friendly excuses for those who insist on organizing children's soccer games on Sunday mornings during the same hours when church school is in session.

The remainder of the Ten Commandments were given by God so that the people of Israel would have some important guidelines for community life. The fifth commandment, "Honor your father and mother" (Exodus 20:12), has been grossly misinterpreted to mean "obey your parents no matter how unreasonable or outrageous this may be." The original intent of this commandment was this: take your parents seriously, give due weight to the lessons to be learned from their life experience, and do not abandon or abuse your parents in their old age when they are vulnerable and unable to be totally productive and independent. Maintaining a healthy relationship and two-way dialogue between older parents and the younger generations was regarded as absolutely essential. Only if the previous heritage of God's covenant was remembered and honored and passed along from one generation to the next, would the people of Israel continue to live in the Promised Land God wanted to give them.

The sixth commandment, "You shall not murder" (Exodus 20:13), maintains that human life is indeed precious to God, and although Israel understood that this commandment applied to respect for life within the community, it did not apply to the people of Israel engaged in warfare and conflict with other peoples in the struggle of Israel to take possession of the Promised Land. The seventh commandment, "You shall not commit adultery" (Exodus 20:14), recognizes that sexuality is a wondrous gift from God but is enormously dangerous and must be upheld within covenantal relations that are life-giving, nurturing, enhancing, and respectful. The eighth commandment, "You shall not steal" (Exodus 20;15), has in mind that a life of dignity for the people of Israel depended upon having certain material goods and possessions in order to thrive and survive, and therefore, it was prohibited for anyone to steal and deprive persons of the essential goods needed for daily living. The ninth commandment, "You shall not bear false witness against your neighbor" (Exodus 20:16), refers specifically to legal testimony in a court of law where it is absolutely necessary that the truth is told and upheld. The tenth commandment, "You shall not covet" (Exodus 20:17), is more specific than prohibiting the simple feeling of desiring something to which you are not entitled. What this commandment has in mind is the destructive desire that results in someone taking action to reach out for something off limits — the neighbor's house, wife, slave, ox, donkey, or anything belonging to the neighbor.

The Ten Commandments are not user friendly in the sense of being easy to follow or easy to apply to the complex and confusing demands of our community responsibilities. There is a wide range of opinions today regarding issues such as what is the proper care of aging parents, whether capital punishment is legalized murder, or what patterns of sexual relationship should be defined as adultery. And so we must let God be God without trying to water down God's demands or to eliminate the growing pains that are essential to achieve spiritual maturity. It's not easy to let go and let God be a God whose "tough love" commandments are designed to bring out the best in us. The Israelites told Moses how terrified they were when God spoke and there was thunder and lightning, the sound of the trumpet, and smoke pouring forth from the mountain. And Moses reassured the people that they should not be afraid because God's "tough love" was intended only to test the people and to put reverent fear and respect in their hearts so that they would not sin. Only when we let God be God will we be in a position to receive the tough love that is not user friendly but indeed is strong enough and truly adequate to bring out the best in us, helping us deal wisely, creatively, and effectively with life's toughest issues and life's most urgent concerns.

---

1. See Walter Brueggemann, *The New Interpreter's Bible, Vol. 1, General And Old Testament Articles, Genesis, Exodus, Leviticus* "The Book of Exodus: Introduction, Commentary, and Reflections" (Nashville: Abingdon Press, 1994), p. 843. "The truth of the matter is that the biblical God is not 'user friendly.'"

Lectionary Preaching After Pentecost

The following index will aid the user of this book in matching the correct Sunday with the appropriate text during Pentecost. All texts in this book are from the series for the First Reading, Revised Common Lectionary. (Note that the ELCA division of Lutheranism is now following the Revised Common Lectionary.) The Lutheran designations indicate days comparable to Sundays on which Revised Common Lectionary Propers or Ordinary Time designations are used.

(Fixed dates do not pertain to Lutheran Lectionary)

Fixed Date Lectionaries *Revised Common (including ELCA) and Roman Catholic*	Lutheran Lectionary *Lutheran*
The Day of Pentecost	The Day of Pentecost
The Holy Trinity	The Holy Trinity
May 29-June 4 — Proper 4, Ordinary Time 9	Pentecost 2
June 5-11 — Proper 5, Ordinary Time 10	Pentecost 3
June 12-18 — Proper 6, Ordinary Time 11	Pentecost 4
June 19-25 — Proper 7, Ordinary Time 12	Pentecost 5
June 26-July 2 — Proper 8, Ordinary Time 13	Pentecost 6
July 3-9 — Proper 9, Ordinary Time 14	Pentecost 7
July 10-16 — Proper 10, Ordinary Time 15	Pentecost 8
July 17-23 — Proper 11, Ordinary Time 16	Pentecost 9
July 24-30 — Proper 12, Ordinary Time 17	Pentecost 10
July 31-Aug. 6 — Proper 13, Ordinary Time 18	Pentecost 11
Aug. 7-13 — Proper 14, Ordinary Time 19	Pentecost 12
Aug. 14-20 — Proper 15, Ordinary Time 20	Pentecost 13
Aug. 21-27 — Proper 16, Ordinary Time 21	Pentecost 14
Aug. 28-Sept. 3 — Proper 17, Ordinary Time 22	Pentecost 15
Sept. 4-10 — Proper 18, Ordinary Time 23	Pentecost 16
Sept. 11-17 — Proper 19, Ordinary Time 24	Pentecost 17
Sept. 18-24 — Proper 20, Ordinary Time 25	Pentecost 18

Sept. 25-Oct. 1 — Proper 21, Ordinary Time 26	Pentecost 19
Oct. 2-8 — Proper 22, Ordinary Time 27	Pentecost 20
Oct. 9-15 — Proper 23, Ordinary Time 28	Pentecost 21
Oct. 16-22 — Proper 24, Ordinary Time 29	Pentecost 22
Oct. 23-29 — Proper 25, Ordinary Time 30	Pentecost 23
Oct. 30-Nov. 5 — Proper 26, Ordinary Time 31	Pentecost 24
Nov. 6-12 — Proper 27, Ordinary Time 32	Pentecost 25
Nov. 13-19 — Proper 28, Ordinary Time 33	Pentecost 26
	Pentecost 27
Nov. 20-26 — Christ the King	Christ the King

Reformation Day (or last Sunday in October) is October 31 (Revised Common, Lutheran)

All Saints' Day (or first Sunday in November) is November 1 (Revised Common, Lutheran, Roman Catholic)

Books In This Cycle A Series

GOSPEL SET

It's News To Me! Messages Of Hope For Those Who Haven't Heard
Sermons For Advent/Christmas/Epiphany
Linda Schiphorst McCoy

Tears Of Sadness, Tears Of Gladness
Sermons For Lent/Easter
Albert G. Butzer, III

Pentecost Fire: Preaching Community In Seasons Of Change
Sermons For Sundays After Pentecost (First Third)
Schuyler Rhodes

Questions Of Faith
Sermons For Sundays After Pentecost (Middle Third)
Marilyn Saure Breckenridge

The Home Stretch: Matthew's Vision Of Servanthood In The End-Time
Sermons For Sundays After Pentecost (Last Third)
Mary Sue Dehmlow Dreier

FIRST LESSON SET

Long Time Coming!
Sermons For Advent/Christmas/Epiphany
Stephen M. Crotts

Restoring The Future
Sermons For Lent/Easter
Robert J. Elder

Formed By A Dream
Sermons For Sundays After Pentecost (First Third)
Kristin Borsgard Wee

Living On One Day's Rations
Sermons For Sundays After Pentecost (Middle Third)
Douglas B. Bailey

Let's Get Committed
Sermons For Sundays After Pentecost (Last Third)
Derl G. Keefer

SECOND LESSON SET
Holy E-Mail
Sermons For Advent/Christmas/Epiphany
Dallas A. Brauninger

Access To High Hope
Sermons For Lent/Easter
Harry N. Huxhold

Acting On The Absurd
Sermons For Sundays After Pentecost (First Third)
Gary L. Carver

A Call To Love
Sermons For Sundays After Pentecost (Middle Third)
Tom M. Garrison

Distinctively Different
Sermons For Sundays After Pentecost (Last Third)
Gary L. Carver

www.ingramcontent.com/pod-product-compliance
Lightning Source LLC
Chambersburg PA
CBHW071735040426
42446CB00012B/2364